CW01111697

JOURNAL OF THE CANADIAN SOCIETY FOR SYRIAC STUDIES

Journal of the Canadian Society for Syriac Studies/ de la Société Canadienne des Études Syriaques

The *JCSSS* is a refereed journal published annually, and it contains the transcripts of public lectures presented at the Society and possibly other articles and book reviews

Editorial Board

General Editor Amir Harrak, *University of Toronto*

Editors

Sebastian Brock, *Oxford University*
Robert Kitchen, Saskatchewan
Craig E. Morrison, *Pontifical Biblical Institute, Rome*
Lucas van Rompay, *Duke University*
Kyle Smith, *University of Toronto*
Alexander Treiger, *Dalhousie University*
Rita Sawaya, *University of Toronto*

Copy Editing Amir Harrak, Rita Sawaya

Publisher

Gorgias Press
180 Centennial Avenue, Suite 3

The Canadian Society for Syriac Studies
La Société Canadienne des Etudes Syriaques

Society Officers 2022-2023

President: Amir Harrak
Vice-President: Khalid Dinno
and Secretary-Treasurer: Arlette Londes

Members of the Board of Directors:

Marica Cassis, Khalid Dinno, Geoffrey Greatrex, Amir Harrak,
Robert Kitchen, Kyle Smith, Ashoor Yousif

The aim of the CSSS is to promote the study of the Syriac culture which is rooted in the same soil from which the ancient Mesopotamian and biblical literatures sprung. The CSSS is purely academic, and its activities include a series of public lectures, one yearly symposium, and the publication of its Journal. The Journal is distributed free of charge to the members of the CSSS who have paid their dues, but it can be ordered by other individuals and institutions through Gorgias Press (www.gorgiaspress.com).

Cover:
Fragment BL Add. MS 17.216, folio 6 rec. (detail), Photo© Rita Sawaya, June, 2023, by Permission from the British Library. (Thanks to Michael Erdman—Head Middle Eastern and Central Asian Collections.)

JOURNAL OF THE CANADIAN SOCIETY FOR SYRIAC STUDIES

Volume 23

GORGIAS PRESS
2023

Copyright © 2023 by The Canadian Society for Syriac Studies.

All rights reserved under International and Pan-American Copyright Conventions. No part of this publication may be reproduced, stored in a retrieval system or transmitted in any form or by any means, electronic, mechanical, photocopying, recording, scanning or otherwise without the prior written permission of Gorgias Press LLC.

Published in the United States of America by Gorgias Press LLC, New Jersey

ISBN 978-1-4632-4619-8

ISSN: 1499-6367

GORGIAS PRESS
954 River Rd., Piscataway, NJ 08854 USA
www.gorgiaspress.com

The paper used in this publication meets the minimum requirements of the American National Standards.

Printed in the United States of America

Table of Contents

From the Editor 1

Sebastian Brock, 3
A Syriac Narrative Concerning the 107
Pythagorean Philosophers and True Silence

Khalid Dinno, 9
The Syriac Orthodox Patriarchal Archives:
Treasures of History and Culture

Duman Riyazi, 21
A Look at One of the First Armenian Plays in Iran

Amir Harrak, 26
Calendar, Popular Medical Prescriptions and
Treatments, and the Zodiac Circle

Rita Sawaya, 33
The Page Layout of a Syriac Fragment: BL Add.
Manuscript 17.216– ff. 2-14

James Toma,
The Mongol Invasion of North Mesopotamia— 47
A Translation and Analysis of Gewargis Warda
On Karamalish

FROM THE EDITOR

This twenty-third volume of JCSSS celebrates doctoral candidates writing about their studies, as well as papers written by officers of the CSSS and an article by a post-doctoral candidate—all with a variety of topics.

Sebastian Brock who is an Editor of the JCSSS is the author of the first article entitled "A Syriac Narrative Concerning the 107 Pythagorean Philosophers and True Silence." This article as part of Brock's recent series of short texts dealing with Classical Greek popular philosophy in manuscript Sinai Syr. 14, with a focus on the '107 Pythagorean philosophers' who maintained silence. Brock demonstrates that although this text seems to be non-extant in Greek, it much certainly must have come from a Greek source.

Dr. Khalid Dinno is the Vice President of the CSSS. His article is entitled "The Syriac Orthodox Patriarchal Archives: Treasures of History and Culture." In this article, Dinno discusses Syriac Orthodox manuscripts of Dayr-al-Za'farān Monastery in Turkey, manuscripts in Amida and Mardīn, as well as Ṭūr-'Abdīn manuscripts—a rich collection that dates back to as early as 740 AD! The archival material surveyed in this paper highlight the richness of the Syriac Orthodox manuscript collections in these holy places.

Duman Riyazi is a Susan Salek Postdoctoral Fellow with the Elahé Omidyar Mir-Djalali Institute of Iranian Studies. His research focuses on manuscripts of the '*commedia del arte*,' and on theatrical relations between East and West. His paper features Armenian manuscripts that show how Western theater was open to the Armenian communities in the Qajar period, through the trade of merchants and with travelers.

Amir Harrak is the Head of the Syriac and Aramaic Program at the University of Toronto's Department of Near and Middle Eastern Civilizations. He is also the founder and president of the Canadian Society for Syriac Studies (CSSS) and JCSSS. His paper "Calendar, Popular Medical Prescriptions and Treatments, and the Zodiac Circle," explores a manuscript owned by the Iraqi Department of Antiquities and Heritage. This article features several topics in this codex, including Zodiac and horoscope, popular remedies in Mesopotamia, popular medicine, calendars, eclipses, intercourse and pregnancy.

Rita Sawaya is a Doctoral Candidate in Syriac and Aramaic Studies, a Teaching Fellow at the Department of Near and Middle Eastern Civilizations, a Research Fellow in Manuscript Studies at the University of Toronto. She has joined CSSS as JCSSS Editor as of 2023. Her work focuses on inter-disciplinary manuscript studies where she explores the materiality of Syriac manuscripts in addition to the traditional philological approach. Her paper, "The Page Layout of Syriac Fragments: BL Add. Manuscript 17.217– ff. 2-14," deals with the layout of a Syriac fragment dated to the 7th century, and the challenges of reconstructing the story of this fragment from damaged, dismembered and rebound folios based on established standards.

James Toma is a Doctoral Candidate in Syriac Studies at the University of Toronto and a Teaching Fellow at the Department of Near and Middle Eastern Civilizations. His article on Giwargis Warda's poetry deals with this author's description of the Mongol invasion of North Mesopotamia. He provides an edition, translation and interpretation of Gewargis' detailed depiction of the massacres in three Chaldean towns in three places of the Nineveh Plains: Karamlish, Beth-Qoqa, and Tell-Esqopa. The aim of this paper is to shed new light on an otherwise obscure period.

Do you know that the CSSS is nearly a quarter of a century old, and its *Journal* JCSSS is almost as old as the CSSS? Both JCSSS and CSSS are part of the Syriac Studies and Aramaic Programme at the University of Toronto.

This year's symposium features a variety of topics related to "Syriac and Syriac and Christian Arabic Literature" with papers by Dr. Sebastian Brock, Dr. Khalid Dinno, Dr. Amir Harrak, Rita Sawaya, Dr. Duman Riyazi, Dr. Adrian Zakar, James Toma and Sihaam Khan.

A. H.

November 2023

A SYRIAC NARRATIVE CONCERNING THE 107 PYTHAGOREAN PHILOSOPHERS AND TRUE SILENCE

SEBASTIAN BROCK
UNIVERSITY OF OXFORD

Pythagoras is chiefly known in Syriac from a collections of 112 Symbols, quoted in a work by the ninth-century Syrian Orthodox writer Theodosius,[1] and from a collection of Sentences.[2] Both works are translations from known Greek texts. The short text published below, preserved in Sinai Syriac 14, will certainly also be a translation from Greek, but this time no corresponding text in Greek seems to survive.

The short opening sentence of the work serves as a descriptive heading to the work: "There once gathered 107 philosophers who observed silence, from the school (lit. teaching) of Pythagoras". As they were meditating in silence on all the vanity and error of the present world, one of their number dropped down dead, whereupon another of them, MRMWLYS, observed to his companions (addressed as "Sages") that, whereas they had been holding on to just the "shadow of silence", their dead companion had taken hold of "true silence". He further comments that this kind of silence, which has no "natural instruction", provides true liberation. He ends with the exhortation to "be like the hare" in the face of vexation, and "if you want to be someone who has no authority above you – like a king– keep at a distance from the company of human beings".

That silence was a subject of importance for Pythagoras is well attested,[3] and according to Iamblichus' *On the Pythagorean Life* (also often known as the *Life of Pythagoras*), it played an important role in the training of his disciples: once someone had been accepted on the basis of a rigorous initial examination, he was sent away and ignored for three years, to test his constancy and his genuine love of learning, and to see whether he had the right attitude to reputation and was able to despise status.

After this (Pythagoras) imposed a five-year silence on this adherent, to test their self-control: control of the tongue, he thought, is the most difficult type of self-control, a truth made apparent to us by those who established the mysteries. During this time, each one's property was held in common, entrusted to particular students who were called "civil servants" and who managed the finances and made the rules. If the candidates were found worthy to share in the teachings, judging by their life and general principles, then after the five-year silence they joined the inner circle.[4]

A distant reflection of this paragraph features in Syriac in the ninth-century Monastic History by Thomas of Marga, who writes:

Pythagoras, the master (*rabba*) of philosophers, having grasped, from the experience (*nesyana*) of considerable time, that without the body being stilled (*meštalyanuta*) in reclusion (*ḥbušya*), and the tongue being silent from speech, philosophy cannot be acquired, he instructed everyone who was undergoing discipleship in his school to maintain silence for five years, and it was from listening and sight that the introduction to wisdom was practiced in the school.[5]

The five-year period of silence was not only just one part of the preparation for initiation into inner secrets of Pythagoras' teaching,[6] but it should also be understood, as Pietro Piro has observed, as in itself a 'ritual death'.[7] That the main aim of the philosophical life was 'meditation on death' (μελέτη θανάτου) is already something specified in Plato's *Phaedo*.[8] This link between silence and death happens to be vividly illustrated in the Syriac text published below.

Whether or not the figure of 107 given for the number of the philosophers is significant, is unclear: while 107 is a prime number, it is not one of the Pythagorean primes (whereas 109 would have been). The identity of MRMWLYS, too, remains uncertain. Since Iamblichus' list of Pythagoreans[9] known to him includes a certain Myllias, one might suggest that the first two letters of MRMWLYS should be taken as representing the honorific MAR(Y), 'my lord', although this would normally be writer MRY.

The transmission: Sinai Syr. 14 [10]

The manuscript can best be categorized as an anthology of (usually) short texts of monastic interest, one of whose distinctive features lies in the inclusion of a number of texts connected with the names of Greek philosophers. The manuscript, whose folios are in some disorder,[11] has been dated to the tenth century; it is written in an early serto script and is certainly of Melkite provenance. The short text published here is to be found on ff. 129v-130r, in a group of other secular texts concerning silence (see below).

The manuscript in its present form opens with an extensive and wide-ranging selection of authors, both Greek and Syriac; the former include not only Makarios,[12] Neilos, John Klimakos, Gregory of Nyssa (On Virginity) and Abba Isaias, but also John Cassian (f. 54v) and John of Carpathus (f.58v), both of whom are very rarely found elsewhere in Syriac. The three Syriac authors included are Isaac of Antioch f. 95v), Isaac of Nineveh (Isaac the Syrian), and Symeon d-Taybutheh ('of the Book of Grace'; f.113r), the last two of whom are both seventh-century monastic authors belonging to the Church of the East.[13]

Following the extract from Symeon comes the first of two groups of texts associated with Greek philosophers:[14]

128rv 'From the philosopher Plato'.[15]

128v-129v 'On Didymus [= Dindamis], a philosopher who was naked and lived in the wilderness'.[16]

129v A short summary of the Life of Secundus the Silent Philosopher.[17]

129v-130r The 107 Pythagorean Philosophers (edited below).

130rv 'Thaumastius [Themistius] the philosopher'. These are excerpts from Themistius' Treatise on Virtue, a work preserved only in Syriac translation.[18]

This group of non-Christian writings is separated from a shorter second group by brief excerpts from Gregory [of Nazianzus]. *Letter* [114] *to Basil*, and Cyril (f. 131rv). This second group consists of:ff. 131v-132r 'From a philosopher'. A short narrative concerning Theon and Symmachus who put questions to Plato.[19]

ff. 132v-133r: 'Stomathalassa the philosopher'.[20]

ff. 133r-135r 'Aristotle the Sage' This turns out to be an abbreviated form of Pseudo- Aristotle, On Virtues and Vices [21].

The remainder of the manuscript contains a very miscellaneous collection of excerpts: the History of John the Little, the History of Dionysius [the Areopagite], Diadochos, Serapion, Mark the Hermit and some further texts, including some attributed to Ephrem. Included among them is a short collection of sayings on the Soul, entitled 'From the Sages' (f. 150v).[22] It might be noted that the folio, in estrangelo, pasted to the wooden back can be identified as coming from Isaac of Nineveh's Second Discourse (ed. Bedjan, pp. 19-20).

TEXT AND TRANSLATION[23]

SYRIAC TEXT

Sinai syr. 14, f.129v-130r

ܒܬܪ ܬܘܒ ܐܬܟܢܫܘ ܡܐܐ ܘܫܒܥܐ ܦܝܠܘܣܘܦܐ
ܢܛܪ̈ܝ ܫܬܩܐ ܡܢ ܝܘܠܦܢܗ ܕܦܝܬܓܘܪܘܣ. ܘܟܕ
ܒܫܬܩܗܘܢ ܬܗܝܪܝܢ ܗܘܘ ܥܠ ܪܗܛܗ ܕܥܠܡܐ
ܗܢܐ. ܘܥܠ ܫܘܚܠܦ̈ܘܗܝ, ܘܥܠ ܣܪܝܩܘܬ ܥܡܠܐ
ܕܥܠ ܐܦ̈ܝ ܗܕܪܗ ܘܐܝܟܘܬܗ . ܘܥܠ ܗܘܦܟܐ
ܘܚܘܕܪܐ ܚܪܝܦܐ ܕܡܟܐܒܢ̈ܘܬܗ ܘܡܚܕ̈ܝܢܘܬܗ
ܕܠܐ ܘܠܝ̈ܬܐ ܝܬܝܪܐܝܬ ܥܠ ܛܥܝܘܬܗܘܢ
ܕܐܝܠܝܢ ܕܪ̈ܕܝܢ ܒܫܘܒܚܐ ܡܬܚܒܠܢܐ. ܘܓܠܝܐܝܬ
ܕܠܐ ܪܓܫܬܐ ܣܚܝܢ ܒܚܛ̈ܗܐ ܕܟܠ
ܐܣܟܝܡ. ܒܝܕ ܥܘܒܝܗ ܕܥܘܬܪܐ ܘܕܫܘܠܛܢܐ.
ܘܥܠ ܣܢܝܩܘܬܗܘܢ ܕܡܝܬܪ̈ܐ. ܘܠܐܘܬܗܘܢ!
ܕܢ̈ܝܚܐ. ܘܥܠ ܫܢܕܗܘܢ ܕܢܟܦ̈ܐ.
ܘܐܘܠܨܢܐ ܕܚܟ̈ܝܡܐ. ܘܚܣܝܪܘܬ ܣܢܝܩܘܬܗܘܢ
ܕܬܪ̈ܝܨܐ. ܘܥܠ ܕܘܘܢܗܘܢ ܕܟܐܒܬܢ̈ܐ ܥܡ
ܕܐܝܟ ܗܠܝܢ.
ܡܢ ܫܠܝ ܕܝܢ ܢܦܠ ܚܕ ܡܢܗܘܢ ܘܡܝܬ. ܥܢܐ ܕܝܢ
ܡܪܡܘܠܝܣ ܘܐܡܪ. ܚܢܢ ܐܘ ܚܟܝ̈ܡܐ ܠܛܠܠܗ
ܕܫܬܩܐ ܐܚܝܕܝܢ ܗܘܝܢ. ܗܐ ܫܢ̈ܝܐ
ܣܓܝ̈ܐܬܐ. ܟܠܢ ܠܦܘܬ ܡܫܘܚܬܐ ܕܕܒܝܐ.
ܒܪܡ ܫܬܩܐ ܫܪܝܪܐ ܗܘܝܘ. ܕܗܢܐ ܚܒܪܢ ܠܒܝܢ.
ܘܥܠ ܗܕܐ ܐܢܐ ܐܡܪ ܐܢܐ. ܕܐܢ ܠܐ ܢܒܕܩ
ܐܢܫ ܠܗܘܢ ܘܒ̈ܥܐ ܕܢܕܪ ܒܫܬܩܘܬܗ
ܒܦܘܪܫܘܬܐ ܕܚܟܡܬܐ. ܐܡܟܢܐ ܕܡܢ ܟܠ
ܗܘܒܪܝܢ ܘܡܢ ܟܠܫ ܢܟܠܐ ܘܢܪܘܚ. ܘܢܬܠܘܗ ܠܟܐ
ܒܫܘܠܡܗ ܠܓܡܪ (130r) ܫܪܪܐ ܕܬܘܕܝܬܐ
ܠܐ ܐܝܟ ܡܥܟܒܢ. ܘܐܦ ܗܫܐ ܐܘ ܚܒܪ̈ܝ. ܠܗ
ܠܫܬܩܐ ܐܫܬܡܥܘܗ ܕܠܝܬ ܡܠܦܢܘܬܐ ܒܢܝܢܬܐ
ܐܟܘܬܗ. ܡܢ ܟܠ ܓܒ̈ܝܢ ܗܘ ܡܟܘܬܪ. ܠܝܬ ܓܝܪ
ܡܕܡ ܒܗܢܐ ܥܠܡܐ ܕܡܝܬܪ ܡܢ ܫܬ̈ܩܘܬܐ
ܐܟܘܬܗ. ܐܦ ܓܝܪ ܠܦܘܬ ܠܟܐ ܕܫܬܝܩܬ
ܘܐܬܚܫܒܬ ܒܥܠܝܠܘܬ ܡܪܕܝܬܗ ܕܒܩܪܐ ܗܢܐ.
ܠܝܬ ܒܚܟܡܬܐ ܕܡܪܕܐ ܐܝܟ ܫܠܝܐ ܡܢ ܟܠ
ܦܘܠܚ̈ܢܐ ܡܬܚܫܒ̈ܢܐ. ܘܫܬܩܐ ܕܡܢ ܡܡܠܠܐ
ܫܘܠܡܗ ܒܗܢܐ ܡܢ ܡܕܒܪܢܘܬܐ ܕܡ̈ܠܠܐ܀
ܡܢ ܟܠܬܐ ܗܘܝ ܐܪܒܥܐ ܗܘܘ ܕܝܢ ܡܢ ܚܟܝܡܐ[24]
ܕܫܡܫܐ ܢܒ̇ܥ ܡܢܗ ܒܪܘܡ. ܘܢܘܗܪܝܢ ܕܣܘܠܛܢܐ
ܐܝܟ ܐܪܒܥܐ. ܘܠܐ ܢܘܗܪܝܢ ܫܡܫܐ. ܐܢ
ܒܪܐ ܐܝܬ ܕܗܘܐ ܕܠܝܬ ܕܫܠܛ ܟܠܝܢ ܐܝܟ
ܡܠܟܐ ܬܬܪܝܣ ܡܢ ܒܪ̈ܢܫܐ܀

TRANSLATION

Next: Once there gathered 107 philosophers who preserved silence, from the school (lit. teaching) of Pythagoras.

While, during their silence, they were (in a state of) wonder at the course of this world and at its changes, at the vanity of toil over its fair adornment, at the turn-around and sharp cycle of its things that improperly cause pain and joy; and especially at the error of those who proceed in corruptible glory and openly, without awareness, bathe n sins of every sort, through the opacity of wealth and authority; and at the need of virtuous people and the weariness of the gentle, and at the misery of the chaste, and the affliction of the prudent, the lack of necessities of the upright and the torment of the sick and those like them: –all if suddenly one of them collapsed and died.

MRMWLYS answered and said, 'We, O Sages, have been holding on to the shadow of silence for many years, each (of us) according to the measure of his time; but this is the true silence, which our companion has taken hold of. And concerning this I say, If someone does not subdue all stirrings of his sense-perception with wisdom's discernment in order to be still and keep distant from every action and every person, and (does not) meditate on his end, he will not find true virtue at all.

'Now too, my companions, I have found (a kind of) silence that has no natural instruction like it: from every aspect it is advantageous, for there is nothing in this habitable (world) like which liberates from griefs. For also, with regard to the heart, I have tested it, and been tested by the swiftness of the course of this habitable (world); there is no choice which benefits as much as does stillness from all works that are subject to corruption, along with silence from talking, for its end is hidden from the knowledge of rational beings. 'In the face of vexation be (like) a hare: that is, flee from any cause from which torment spring. People will call you timorous,[25] like a hare, but they will not call you (a source of) disturbance. If you want to be someone who has no authority above you, like a king, keep at a distance from the company of human beings.'

NOTES

[1] Ed. H. Zotenberg, 'Les sentences symboliques de Théodose', *Journal asiatique* VII.8 (1876), 425-76; a shorter, but overlapping, collection was published by G. Levi della Vida, 'Sentenze pitagoriche in versione siriaca', *Rivista degli studi orientalli 3* (1910), 595-610 (reprinted in R. Contini (ed.), *Giorgio Levi della Vida, Pitagora, Bardesane e altri studi siriaci* (Rome, 1989). .Cf. A. Izdebska, 'Pythagore dans la tradition syriaque et arabe', in R. Goulet (ed.), *Dictionnaire des phlilosophes antiques* 7 (2018), 867-884, and *eadem*, 'The Riddles of Pythagoras. Arabic and Syriac Symbola attributed to Pythagoras and Socrates', in C. Macris and L. Brisson (eds), *Pythagoras Redivivus. Studies on the Texts attributed to Pythagoras and the Pythagoreans* (Berlin, 2021), 475-509.

[2] Ed. P. de Lagarde, *Analecta Syriaca* (1858; repr. Osnabruck, 1967), 195-201. The Greek original was edited by H. Chadwick in an Appendix to his edition of *The Sentences of Sextus* (Cambridge, 1959), 84-94. A summary of 'the Teaching of Pythagoras' is to be found in Theodore bar Koni, *Liber Scholiorum* (ed. A. Scher, CSCO 69), II, 291-2; the passage was discussed by A. Baumstark, 'Griechische Philosophen und ihre Lehren in syrischer Überlieferung', *Oriens Christianus* 5 (1905), 1-25. Cf. Y. Arzhanov, *Syriac Sayings of Greek Philosophers* (CSCO Subsidia 138; 2019), 84-90.

[3] A survey is given in O. Casel, *De philosophorum graecorum silentio mystico* (Giessen, 1919), with pp. 34-40 on Pythagoras.

[4] Tr. Gillian Clark, *Iamblichus: On the Pythagorean Life* (Liverpool, 1989), §72 (p. 31). G. Staab, in his detailed study of Iamblichus's work, *Pythagoras in der Spätantike* (Berlin, 2012), has no specific comment on the passage (p. 308). The five-year period of silence is also specified in Diogenes Laertius, *Lives of the Philosophers* VIII.10.

[5] Ed. E.A.W. Budge, *The Book of Governors: The Historia Monastica of Thomas Bishop of Marga A.D. 840,* I (London, 1893), Book V.13, p. 297 (lines 15-20); cf. also p. cxix,

[6] For a brief description, see S. Montiglio, *Silence in the Land of Logos* (Princeton, 2000), 27-28.

[7] P. Piro, 'Struttura e significato del silenzio nel rituale di iniziazione pitagorica: il silenzio come morte rituale', *Studia Patavina* 52:1 (2005), 127-148, esp. 137-9.

[8] Plato, *Phaedo,* 80E. As P. Jordan OSB pointed out in his study 'Pythagoras and Monasticism', *Traditio* 17 (1961), 432-441, here 237, 'It seems, then, to be one's chief task in life to prepare for death'.

[9] Iamblichus, *On the Pythagorean Life* §267; he is amongst those listed as coming from Kroton, and his wife, Timycha, is included among the famous Pythagorean women (§§ 189, 192-4).

[10] Cf. P. Géhin, *Les manuscrits syriaques de parchemin du Sinaï et leurs membra disjecta* (CSCO Subsidia 136; Leuven, 2017), 49-50; Arzhanov, *Syriac Sayings*, 41-43.

[11] The first two Quires of the original manuscript are missing, and Quires 4-7 have been displaced: they are now to be found after Quire 10 (which ends on present f.47); thus ff.48-55 are the original Quire 4, etc.; Quire 11 begins on f. 65. Similarly Quire 23 (= present ff. 94-101) is misplaced, having been put after Quire 13. Quire 22 (which ends on f.164) is followed on f.165-172 by Quire 25!

[12] Ed. W. Strothmann, *Die syrische Überlieferung der Schriften des Makarios,* (GOFS 21; Wiesbaden, 1981), I. *Syrischer Text* 259-359; II. *Übersetzung*, 181-289.

[13] Part I of Isaac's Discourses were translated into Greek at the Monastery of St Sabbas, near Jerusalem, c. 800, and have ever since proved very popular monastic reading in the (Chalcedonian) Orthodox tradition; The extracts in Sinai Syr. 14 come from both Part I (ff. 65r-93v) and Part II (ff. 119r-128r).

[14] An earlier text of philosophical content is to be found on f. 101rv, 'On philosophy', which can be identified as part of the *Definitions of Philosophy* attributed to Michael Badoqa; for further details see . S.P. Brock, 'Some Syriac pseudo-Platonic curiosities', in R. Hansberger, A. al-Akiti, and C. Burnett (eds), *Medieval Arabic Thought. Essays in Honour of Fritz Zimmermann* (Warburg Institute Studies and Texts 4; 2012), 19-26, here 19-20.

[15] Ed. with English translation in Brock, 'Some Syriac pseudo-Platonic curiosities', 21-23. Cf. Arzhanov, *Syriac Sayings*, 77-79.

[16] Ed with English translation in Brock, 'Stomathalassa, Dandamis and Secundus in a Syriac monastic anthology', in G.J. Reinink and A.C. Klugkist (eds), *After Bardaisan. Studies on Continuity and Change in Syriac Christianity in Honour of Professor Han J.W. Drijvers* (Orientalia Lovaniensia Analecta 89; 1999), 35-50, here 40-46. Cf. Arzhanov, *Syriac Sayings*, 102-103.

[17] Ed. with English translation in Brock, 'Stomathalassa', 47-48. Cf. Arzhanov, *Syriac Sayings*, 100-102.

[18] For the passages, see Brock, 'Stomathalassa', 49. An Italian translation of the Syriac version is provided by M. Conterno, *Temistio orientale* (Brescia, 2014).

[19] Ed. with English translation in Brock, 'Some Syriac pseudo-Platonic curiosities', 23-24.

[20] Ed. with English translation in Brock, 'Stomathalassa', 37-40. Cf. Arzhanov, *Syriac Sayings*, 98-100.

[21] Ed. with English translation in Brock, 'An abbreviated Syriac version of Ps. Aristotle, *de Virtutibus et Vitiis*, and *Divisiones*', in E. Coda and C. Martini Bernadeo (eds), *De l'Antiquité tardive au Moyen Âge. Études de logique aristotélienne et de philosophie grecque , syriaque, arabe et latine offertes à Henri Hugonnard-Roche* (Paris, 2014), 91-112.

[22] For this and other related collections, see Arzhanov, *Syriac Sayings*, 42-3.

[23] I am most grateful to the Holy Monastery of St Catherine, Mount Sinai, for permission to publish this text.

[24]Ms ܒܥܬܐ

[25] The timidity of hares is proverbial; in Syriac, see Anton of Tagrit, *The Fifth Book of Rhetoric* (ed. J.W. Watt; CSCO 480; 1986), 68, lines 13-14 (an unidentified saying cited alongside some Sayings of Pythagoras).

THE SYRIAC ORTHODOX PATRIARCHAL ARCHIVES: TREASURES OF HISTORY AND CULTURE

KHALID DINNO
CANADIAN SOCIETY FOR SYRIAC STUDIES

INTRODUCTION

The early cultural identity of the Syrian Orthodox may be characterized and expressed by the works of the highly prominent poet-theologians Ephrem the Syrian (d. 373), Jacob of Sarug (d. 521), the exegete Philoxenus of Mabug (d. 523), the mathematician and astronomer Severus Sābokht (d. 666), the theologian, exegete grammarian, philosopher and historian Jacob of Sarug (d. 708) and George bishop of the Arab (d. 724). This identity continued to be confirmed by the works of subsequent scholars that came who included Anṭūn of Takrit (9th century), the exegete Moshē Bar-Kīphā (d. 903) and also featured two early prominent chronicles: the *Chronicle of Zuqnīn* (written in 775/6) and the non-extant *Ecclesiastical History* of Dionysius of Tell-Maḥrē (d. 845), whose contents survived in extensive quotations in the *Chronical of Michael the Syrian* (d. 1199).The list of prominent literary works also includes the *Chronical 1234* by who came to be known as *"the Anonymous Edessan,"* whose last contribution in the chronical was in the year 1234[1]. This memorable period of cultural contribution was highlighted by the contributions of the renowned theologian and philosopher Bar-Hebraeus (d. 1286), author of thirty-five literary works that include his renowned *General* and *Ecclesiastical Chronicles*. However, concurrent with that period and indeed over the course of the twelfth century the Abbasid Caliphate was undergoing serious decline that was associated with the dominance of the Turkish Saljuqs and the Zangi Atabegs and subsequently aggravated by the arrival of the Mongols, starting with their invasion of Baghdad in 1258. The subsequent decline worsened when Tamerlane ransacked Baghdad and the entire region in 1392-1393. As a result, most regions and towns were devastated, including such major towns Amid, Mardīn, Erbil, Mosul and the major region of Ṭūr-Abdīn. Further, this entire region and beyond was subsequently ruled by Tamerlane's vassals: the Qara-Qoyunlu and the Aq-Qoyunlu until 1508 when the Ottoman sultan Selim-1 brought the entire region under the more stable Ottoman rule. By this time, however, a great number of churches and monasteries had been subject to partial or even total ruin and the archival heritage preserved in them perished. Further, despite the much needed relative peace that was brought in by the Ottoman rule, the cultural decline generally continued, with recovery remaining minor, until the end of the Ottoman period.

During the noted periods of decline considerable amounts of archival material perished, although many did survive in churches and in monasteries. Considerable effort has been underway over the past few decades to preserve and protect what survived of this rich archival heritage.

ARCHIVAL HERITAGE AND SOURCES

The archival heritage of the Syriac Orthodox Church has, over the past few centuries, been preserved in part in many museums and archival centres in Europe, the Vatican, in particular, in America in addition to the Middle East. Naturally, the main source of most of the archives has always been the Middle East, principally Turkey, where the majority of the Syriac Orthodox lived over most of the past few centuries until WWI. Other important Middle Eastern sources include Iraq, Syria, Palestine, particularly Jerusalem, Lebanon and Egypt. For archival sources from Syria and Jerusalem, in particular, see Dinno.[2] The purpose of this article is to shed broad light on the archival heritage of this church, which is grouped here into the following three categories:

i: Liturgical and related cultural archives.

ii: General Church and community related archives.

iii: Church dioceses and related historical records.

I. LITURGICAL AND RELATED CULTURAL ARCHIVES

The material related to this major, indeed most significant category discussed here has generally and historically been preserved in Syriac Orthodox monasteries and churches, whether major or minor. A major, indeed unparalleled, search, study and documentation of this heritage was carried out by Aphrām Barsoum, the well-known Twentieth Century patriarch of the Syriac Orthodox Church, when he was a young monk in Deir al-Za'farān (*Dayrō-d-Kurukmō*) during the first decade of the twentieth century[3]. Barsoum's research covered most regions of Turkey where most the Syriac Orthodox lived during the Ottoman period. The outcome of Barsoum's unique and timely extensive search and research has relatively recently (in 2008) been published by the Syriac Orthodox Patriarchate in three large volumes each comprising around 500 pages. These volumes cover the following three major historical church domains:

A) The Deyr-a-Za'farān[4] Manuscripts. See the volume's front cover in Figure Figure 1.1.

B) The Āmida and Mardīn Manuscripts.

C) The Ṭūr-Abdīn Manuscripts.

Samples of Manuscripts covered by the above referenced publications:

- The Dayr al-Za'farān (=Dayrō-d-Kurukmō) Manuscripts. Due to space limitations, only an archival sample of page 399 of the document is shown here, see Figure 1.2. This informs that this document, dated to AD 687, was written on parchment. Figure 1.3 shows a page of text in Aphrām's handwriting.
- The Omid (=Amida) and Mardīn Manuscripts. As a sample, page 390, shown in Figure 1.4, denotes a date of inscription of 1471 AD.
- The Ṭūr-Abdīn Manuscripts. This is the richest collection of the manuscripts addressed here. The book describes manuscripts that dates back to as early as 740

AD (p. 84)—see Figures 1.5—to 793 AD p. 170), to 855 AD (p. 218), to 1203 AD (p. 185), to 1405 AD (p. 147), to 1489 AD (p. 384) and to 1643 AD (p. 418).

However, as is sadly known, the region under reference in Turkey underwent considerable destruction and its population was subjected in 1915 to a genocide that came to be known as *Sayfo*. An account of what survived of this heritage is currently under study by the Patriarchate of the Syriac Orthodox Church. However, regardless of the outcome of such a study, the precious literature covered by these archives provides a clear vision of the archival heritage of the Syriac Orthodox Church during the post-Abbasid era. In this regard, the following is quoted from the Preface of the volume containing the "Dayr-al-za'farān Manuscripts," written by the Late Patriarch Ignatius Zakka I Iwas:[5]

> ...we have consecrated the first volume of the manuscripts found in the churches of Ṭūr-Abdīn and this second volume contains those manuscripts found in the library of Al-Za'farān Monastery. The scientific and historical worth of these manuscripts has multiplied and, in particular, their value increased after losing most of them through the persecutions and massacres that assaulted the Syriac Church in the region, whereby a great number of those documents was lost. Hence, this present index has become the best and the sole reference for scientists and researchers regarding our precious manuscripts that once existed in that area.

D) The manuscripts that have been in a better environment for survival are those related to the historically famous Fourth Century monastery of Mār-Matta, located approximately 20 kms to the northeast of Mosul, and to the nearby relatively close small towns that constitute the Mār-Mattai's Diocese. These manuscripts are described in a book entitled *Fahāris al-Makhṭūṭāt al-Suryāniyyā fī Abrashiyāt Dayr Mār-Mattā*, published in 2010 by Ghānim al-Shamānī. The referenced book covers the manuscripts in the following locations: the Mar Matti Monastery and churches in the churches of the five towns located close to the monastery, namely: Mōr-Zakai in the town of Mergī; Mart-Shmūnī in Ba'shīqā, Mōr-Jarjīs in Bahazani, Mart-Shmūnī in Bartilla and al-'Adhrā (the Virgin) in Bartilla. A total of 450 manuscripts are referenced in this book.

It is important to note here that another major source of manuscripts and church records in northern Iraq is related to the major historical city of Mosul, whose churches include the historic Fourth Century Church of Mār-Tūmā. However, as we sadly know this city was invaded by ISIS in 2014, which expelled all Christians from this major city in a historically unprecedented act of evil. All church fathers of this city found themselves in urgent need to save and run away with what they could of records and heritage material to safe locations. What has been saved is still largely unspecified.

II. GENERAL CHURCH AND COMMUNITY RELATED ARCHIVES

This is an important sector of church history as, in the broad sense, the church lives through its people. Archives that specifically include letters from community members to church leadership were likely to be common in many if not most dioceses. However, attention will be concentrated here on the archives at the Monastery of Deir al-Za'farān and the Church of the Forty Martyrs in Mardīn, where, historically, important findings have recently been uncovered and addressed.

Being the seat of the patriarchate of the Syriac Orthodox Church for nearly seven centuries, Deir al-Za'farān was the main depository of church documents that included a large proportion of church community correspondence with church leadership, particularly the patriarch for a long time. However, due to the ravages of time, particularly due to the repeated Kurdish incursions, this monastery lost some of its library material as well as an unknown proportion of its archival material. An evidence of this may be cited from what Horatio Southgate[6], a renowned mid nineteenth century researcher and traveler, noted in his book *Narrative of a Visit to the Syrian (Jacobite) Church of Mesopotamia*, published in 1840. He reported that when he wished to visit the Deir al-Za'farān monastery's historic library, the bishop who accompanied him apologized for the library's depleted contents, as:

> "the Kurds had used most of the ancient codices as wadding for their guns during their last occupation of the establishment."

However, despite such losses, a great wealth of surviving archival material was accessed over the period 2005-2010. Most of the imaging (copying) work was carried out in July 2010 by a team that included George Kiraz and this author. myself. Earlier imaging work of some of the material at Deir al-Za'farān monastery had been carried out in 2005 and 2007 by a team that was headed by George Kiraz. All material had been stored without being catalogued. The total imaging work carried out over these three years totaled nearly 19,000 images. Deir al-Za'farān , as we know, was the seat of the patriarch of the SOC from the early 13th century to 1924. Most of these archives covered correspondence to and from the patriarch over a period of time that spanned more than a century, beginning from the early 1820s[7].

A good proportion of this archival material consisted of letters addressed to the patriarch of the day from a variety of sources from within the church hierarchy as well as from the community, in addition to a good measure from outside sources. A sample of these letters is attached, see Figures 2.1 and 2.2.

Characteristics of the Letters to the Patriarch: Format and Contents

1. Period and Document Dating

The period covered by the archival material relates to the period of leadership of the following patriarchs:

Elias II (1838-1847); Jacob II (1847-1871);

Peter III/IV (1872-1894); Abdul Masih II (1895-1903);

Abdullah II (1906-1915); Elias III (1917- 1932).

Concerning document dating, two dating systems were in use until 1840: the *Gregorian* for general internal correspondence and *Hijri* for correspondence with government. However, as part of the 1839 *Tanzimat* reforms, the Ottomans used the *Rumi* calendar when referring to civic matters. The Rumi calendar, which had a Julian year length, was adopted on March 30, 1840.

2. Language and Content

The majority of the documents were written in either of the following: Ottoman Turkish, Arabic, colloquial Syriac, or Garshuni (generally Arabic, but also Turkish in Syriac script). Few documents, generally from India or from European countries, were written in English, and even still fewer in Armenian. Generally, about 20% of the letters were in Arabic, 27% in Ottoman Turkish, 51% in Syriac script (Garshuni) (2-3% in the Syriac language and 48-49% in slang Syriac (Ṭūrōyō), and approximately 2% in English and other languages[8]. The wide use of Garshuni may be attributed to the appreciation and reverence that people held to Syriac language in which the Garshuni is penned. It may also be attributed to the fact that it offered privacy compared to other generally recognized writing formats. However, in Mosul as well as in the small towns surrounding it, Arabic was the main language of communication, supplemented in some of the small towns by colloquial Syriac.

Concerning content, as one might expect, the letters dealt with a variety of topics. Some were of administrative nature, from local bishops, heads of monasteries, priests, monks, and wardens responsible for collecting fifes and patriarchal dues. However, a good proportion of the letters to the patriarch came from individuals or groups of individuals who wished to express concerns or complaints about issues affecting the life of the church community, including the appointment of clergy, or to plead for help in dealing with government authorities, or to report aggression by neighbouring Muslim communities. The large volume of letters from individuals came mainly from the community in Turkey, likely due to closer geography. The wide range of topics addressed in the letters demonstrates that the patriarchate was readily accessible to ordinary individuals. Yet, at the same time, the reverential manner in which the letters were written reflect the esteem with which the patriarch was held in the minds and hearts of his people, not only as their highest ecclesiastical leader, but also as their protector and father.

III. CHURCH DIOCESES AND RELATED HISTORICAL RECORDS

An overview of the demographic distribution of the Syriac Orthodox communities in the early 1870s is given in two Syriac manuscripts in the Mingana Collection (Birmingham) dated 1872.[9] The referenced distribution includes 23 dioceses with a total population of 237,880.

A much greater and more extensive source of information relating to church dioceses will be found in the 467 folio manuscript collection dated 1924 that was penned by Barsoum and is briefly addressed here. Barsoum collected and compiled this huge data from his research and travels throughout Turkey, Iraq and Greater Syria while he was a monk at Deir al-Zaʻfarān before World War I, as well as in the course of his subsequent extensive research over the following years. This unique manuscript, which is penned essentially in Arabic but with several contents in Syriac, provides information related to the diocese structure of the Syriac Orthodox Church from the early days of the Christian era down to recent times[10]. Barsoum published some of his findings that covered most of the seventeenth and eighteenth centuries in *the Patriarchal Journal* from 1939 to 1941[11]. Patriarch Zakka Iwas published more in the same journal starting from 1981. However, there is still an enormous amount of material, particularly relating to the Syriac dioceses during the earlier centuries, which remain unpublished. The purpose of this brief review is to shed somewhat more light on this very extensive and rich manuscript and on its unique characteristics.

Barsoum divided the Syriac dioceses that existed over the Syriac Orthodox Church history into eight groups comprising a total of nearly 180 dioceses. For each diocese Barsoum provided available and extensively researched information as to the line of metropolitans who served that diocese as well as critical historical events that occurred throughout the history of that diocese and for which the diocese and its bishop were associated or of which they were witness.

This unique historical account goes back to early Christianity. As an example, in the case of the Diocese of Jerusalem, the line of archbishops commences with Jacob, brother of our Lord Jesus, who was Jerusalem`s first metropolitan, and proceeds over the centuries to 1924, the date of the manuscript.

The dioceses in this manuscript are divided into eight geographically based groups, reflecting the extent of the church's geographic spread. This document shows that the largest number of dioceses existed during the early and middle Abbasid period. The manuscript provides the names of the bishops who served in each diocese over the course of history of that diocese, in addition to liturgical information related to or derived from the works of clergy serving those dioceses. In essence, this document serves as a supplementary, but perhaps also in many cases a unique, account of the church`s ecclesiastical history. Reviewing the contents of this document shows that it has been based on data from various sources, including the historic information in the *Chronicle of Michael the Syrian* (d. 1199), which includes the valuable work of Dionysius of Tel-Mahre (d. 845), the *Ecclesiastical Chronicle of Bar Hebraeus* (d. 1286), and others that also include a wide range of foreign sources. Due to space restrictions, only few examples, which are related to a number of particularly historically significant dioceses, have been selected from this manuscript for this brief publication.

The Diocese of Jerusalem: Thirty-nine pages of this manuscript are devoted to this historically significant diocese, whose first bishop was Jacob, brother of our Lord Jesus (page 2 of manuscript). The following particularly note-worthy historical facts are stated here: Page 4 of the referenced manuscript, see Figure 3.1, addresses bishops numbers 33 to 48 for the period from 221 to 421 AD. This manuscript, among other historical facts, notes that Bishop Makarius, (bishop number 43) who served from 313 to 335 AD, attended the Council of Nicaea in 325 AD, accompanied by 18 bishops from Palestine. It also notes that Bishop Kirillus I, who served from 350 to 386 AD was temporarily expelled by the Aeriusians. It also notes that Bishop Kirillus II attended the Council of Constantinople in 381 AD, accompanied by 8 bishops from Palestine.

Page 14 of the referenced manuscript, see Figure 3.2, addresses bishops number 78 from around 1080 AD to bishop Athanasius Saliba, brother of Patriarch Michael the Great, number 85 to 1190 AD. The side notes in this manuscript with references to sources from Paris and Cambridge, gives typical evidence of the extensive research that was undertaken by Aphrām Barsoum in preparing this manuscript.

Page 18 of the referenced manuscript, see Figure 3.3, addresses bishops Nos. 103 to 109. The bishop, serial number 108, namely Mor-Gregorius Abdul-Jalil al-Mawṣillī, merits a special mention. During the critical time with the Portuguese invasion of India and their attempt to undermine the existing historic Syriac heritage in that country, this bishop's journey to India in 1666 was critical in preserving that heritage.[12]

The Diocese of Amid (Diyar-Bakir): A sample of the 12-page manuscript is given here in the form of a copy of page No. 39, see Figure 3.4. This page addresses several bishops including Simon I who attended the Council of Nicaea in 325 AD, Bishop Mari who attended the Council of Constantinople in 381 AD. It also includes a reference to Bishop Simon II who attended the Council of Ephesus in 431 AD.

The Diocese of Edessa (Urhoy in classical Syriac and Urfa in Turkish): This was a diocese that at the height of its famous history embraced 36 churches and monasteries. It was historically one of the most important cities and cultural centres in the history of the Syriac Orthodox Church. This history is reflected in Manuscripts 327 to 352 of the subject document. A sample manuscript (Manuscript No. 327) is presented here in Figure 3.5, which among other historical facts, quotes Michael the Syrian, in naming the fifteen churches that were destroyed in this city during the rule of the Muslim Arabs.

The Diocese of the Mōr-Matta Monastery: This monastery, located on a mountain to the east of Mosul, has until the present day, been a famous docile centre since the Fourth Century. Manuscript No. 304, shown here in Figure 3.6, names Bishop Barsoum as being its first bishop who was assassinated by Barsoum of Nisibis in 480 AD. Its history is briefly summarized in Manuscripts 304 to 307.

The Diocese of Taghlib: Manuscript No. 193, see Figure 3.7. The Taghlibites were an Arab tribe whose main base was in the south of Najd, who had the following bishops:

1. Daoud, who was bishop of the Arabs in Jazeera and Mosul.
2. Othman, the bishop of Taghalis, who attended the Tikrit Synod in 834 AD.
3. Down to Yūḥannā, who attended the Mār-Mattai Synod in 628 AD.

CONCLUSION

The archival material presented here adds to the existing archival wealth of the Syriac Orthodox heritage that has been preserved in significant heritage centres and museums throughout the World. This additional material has included three categories: the first related to liturgical culture, compiled by Aphrām Barsoum in the early years of the 20th Century; the second related to general church and community archival material uncovered in the early 21st Century; and the third, a more recently uncovered group, related to archival history of church dioceses. This third group, compiled by Aphrām Barsoum, and dated 1924, is still largely in a preliminary stage of utilization and invites for a more detailed research into this very important branch of church heritage.

NOTES

[1] The *Anonymous Edessan* Chronicle informs that its author was in Jerusalem when Ṣalaḥ-al-Dīn al-Ayyūbī entered Jerusalem.

[2] Dinno, *The Syrian Orthodox Christians in the Late Ottoman Period and Beyond, Crisis Then Revival* (New Jersey: Gorgias Press, 2017).

[3] In 1905, Ayyūb Barsoum from Mosul, a young man of 18, joined Deir al-Za'farān, was tonsured a monk in 1907 and named Aphrām and a priest-monk in 1908.

[4] More usually written as Deir al-Za'farān

[5] Patriarch Ignatius Zakkā I Iwas, *Deyrulza'farān Manuscripts* (Bāb-Tūmā Press, Syria, 2008).

[6] Southgate. *Narrative of a Visit to the Syrian (Jacobites) Church of Mesopotamia.*

[7] Dinno, Khalid. "Accessing the Archival Heritage of the Syrian Orthodox Church;" *Journal of the Canadian Society for Syriac Studies* 13 (2013), pp. 88-94.

[8] Dinno, Khalid. "The Deir-al-Za'faran and Mardin Garshuni Archives." *Hugoye: Journal of Syriac Studies* 17/2 (2014), pp. 195-213.

[9] Presented in TABLE 7 of Brock and Witakowski's *Hidden Pearls, Vol. III: At the Turn of the Third Millennium, The Syrian Orthodox Witness.*

[10] Yūḥannā Ibrāhīm, then the Metropolitan of Aleppo, had a copy of this manuscript, which he was kind enough to permit a photocopy of it to be made for me in July 2010.

[11] Aphrām I Barsoum, *History of the Syriac Dioceses*, edited by George Kiraz (Gorgias Press, 2009); Aphrām I Barsoum, *The Collected Historical Essays of Aphrām I Barsoum*, translated by Matti Moosa (Gorgias Press, 2009).

[12] Dinno, Khalid. "Arabic Documents in the Syriac Orthodox Church Since the Late Ottoman Period." *Journal of the Canadian Society for Syriac Studies* 22 (2022), pp. 3-28.

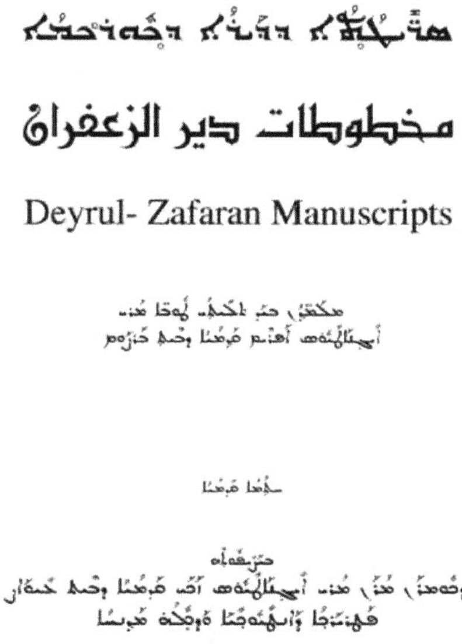

Figure 1.1: Title Page of Manuscript Documents

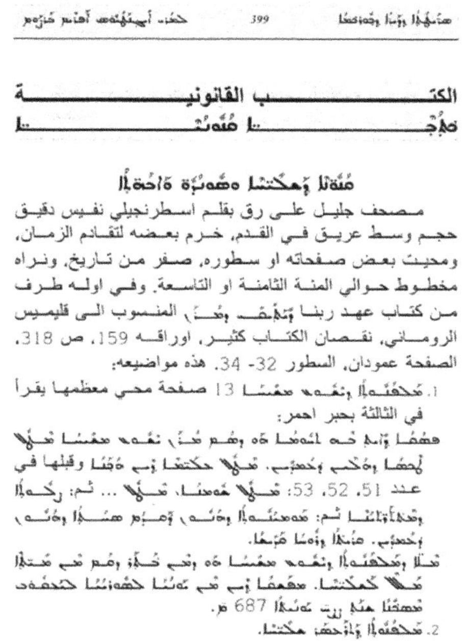

Figure 1.2: Pages 399 of "Deyrul-Zafaran Manuscript," dated to AD 687

Figure 1.3 Inscriptions related to Qal'at Mara in "Omis & Mardin Manuscript" in Aphram Barsoum's Hamdwriting

Figure 1.3 BIS

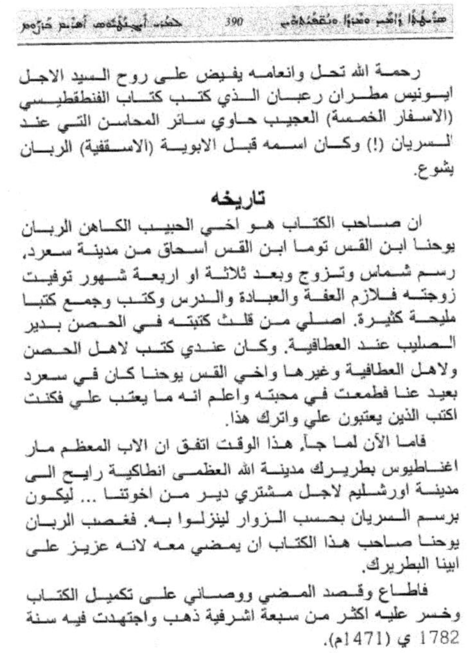

390

رحمة الله تحل وانعامه يفيض على روح السيد الاجل ايونيس مطران رعبان الذي كتب كتاب الفنطقطيسي (الاسفار الخمسة) العجيب حاوي سائر المحاسن التي عند السريان (!) وكان اسمه قبل الابوية (الاسقفية) الربان يشوع.

تاريخه

ان صاحب الكتاب هو اخي الحبيب الكاهن الربان يوحنا ابن القس توما ابن القس اسحاق من مدينة سعرد، رسم شماس وتزوج وبعد ثلاثة او اربعة شهور توفيت زوجته فلازم العفة والعبادة والدرس وكتب وجمع كتبا مليحة كثيرة. اصلي من قلث كتبته في الحصن بدير الصليب عند العطاقية. وكان عندي كتب لاهل الحصن ولاهل العطافية وغيرها واخي القس يوحنا كان في سعرد بعيد عنا فطمعت في محبته واعلم انه ما يعتب علي فكنت اكتب الذين يعتبون علي واترك هذا.

فاما الآن لما جاء هذا الوقت اتفق ان الاب المعظم مار اغناطيوس بطريرك مدينة الله العظمى انطاكية رايح الى مدينة اورشليم لاجل مشتري دير من اخوتنا ... ليكون برسم السريان بحسب الزوار لينزلوا به. فغصب الربان يوحنا صاحب هذا الكتاب ان يمضي معه لانه عزيز على ابينا البطريرك.

فاطاع وقصد المضي ووصاني على تكميل الكتاب وخسر عليه اكثر من سبعة اشرفية ذهب واجتهدت فيه سنة 1782 ي (1471م).

Figure 1.4: Page 390 of the "Omid & Mardin Manuscript" dated to AD 1471

84

[illegible]

الكتابات المزبورة في كنائس حاح

وفي باب مذبح دير مار يوحنا ويسمونه اليوم (دير صور) مزبور سطران بقلم اسطرنجلي وهما اقدم اثر تاريخي في طور عبدين لا يكاد يقرأ منه الا بعض الحروف

[illegible]

اي انه نقش سنة 740 م والبطريرك اثناسيوس الثالث، ولعازر اسقف طورعبدين (740 م 744م) وهذا الاثر خلا سنة كتاب الرسوم السامية لبونيون، وفي باصلوث كنيسة مار سابا العظيمة التي لا تزال اطلالها الضخمة ماثلة ترى هذه الرسوم:

[illegible]

1135 م.

[illegible]

(1175 م).

Figure 1.5: Page of Makhtutat Tur Abdin" dated to AD 770, 1135, and 1175

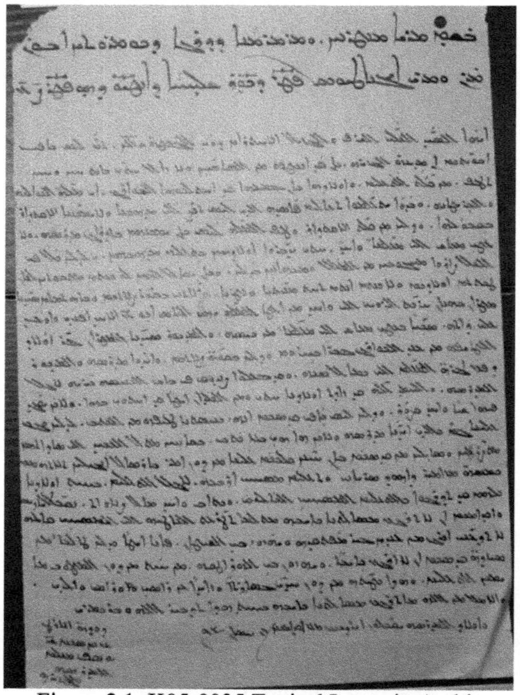

Figure 2.1: K05-0035 Typical Letter in Arabic Garshuni from an Individual to Patriarch Peter III, Dated to April 11. 1893

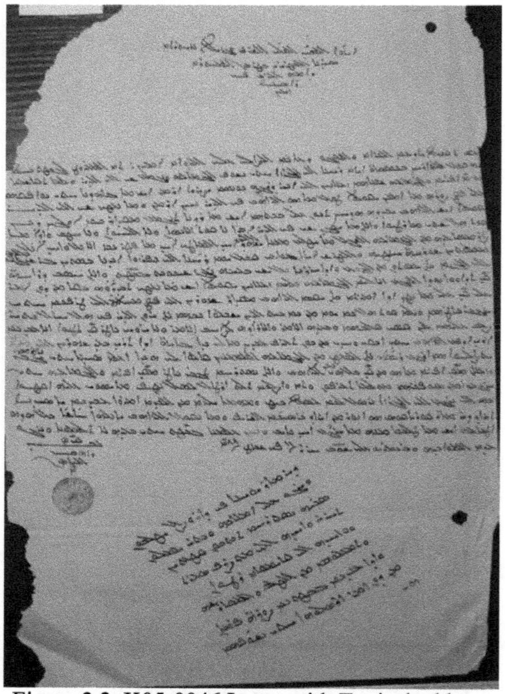

Figure 2.2: K05-0046 Letter with Typical address format, Patriarch Peter III. Dated to April 11, 1888

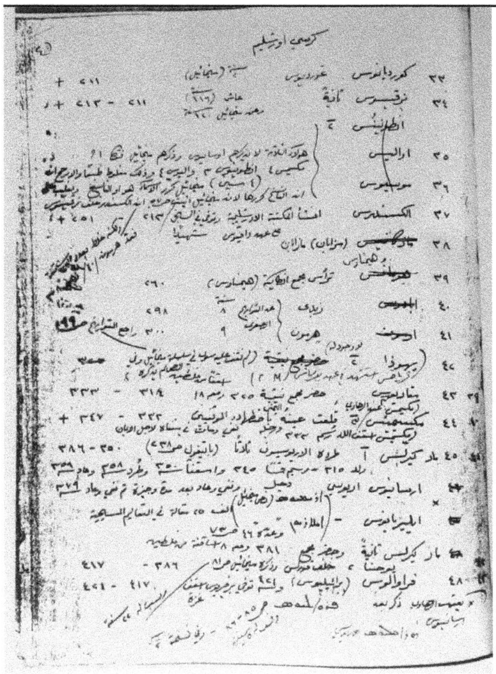

Figure 3.1: Page 4 of Barsoum's Diocese Manuscript Related to the Diocese of Jerusalem

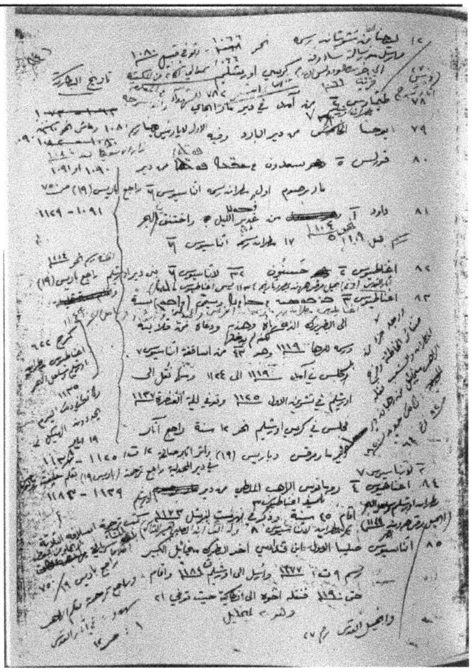

Figure 3.2: Page 14 of Barsoum's Diocese Manuscript Related to the Diocese of Jerusalem

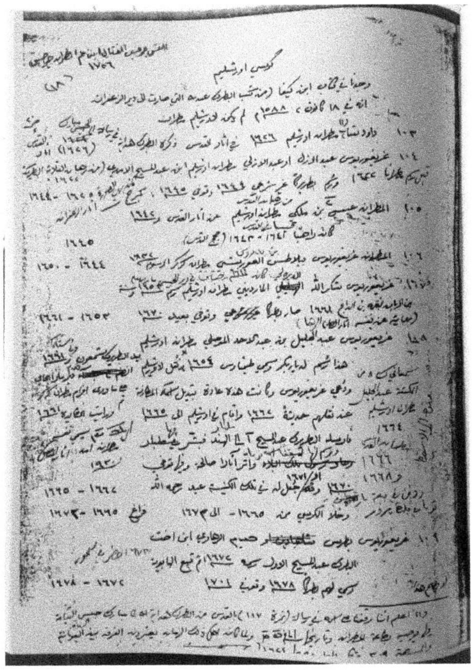

Figure 3.3: Page 18 of Barsoum's Diocese Manuscript Related to the Diocese of Jerusalem

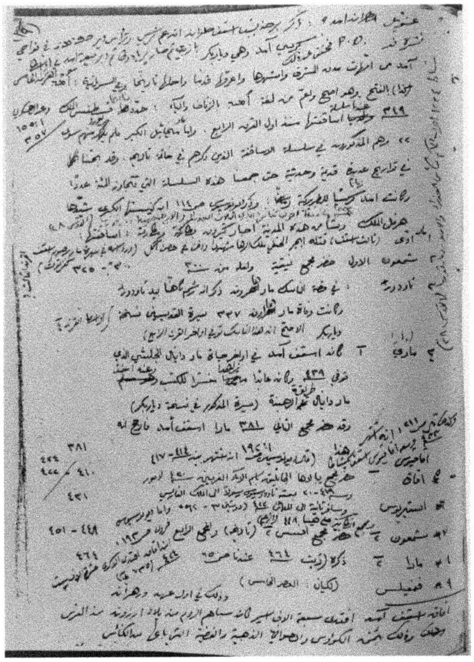

Figure 3.4: Page 39 of Barsoum's Diocese Manuscript Related to the Diocese of Amida

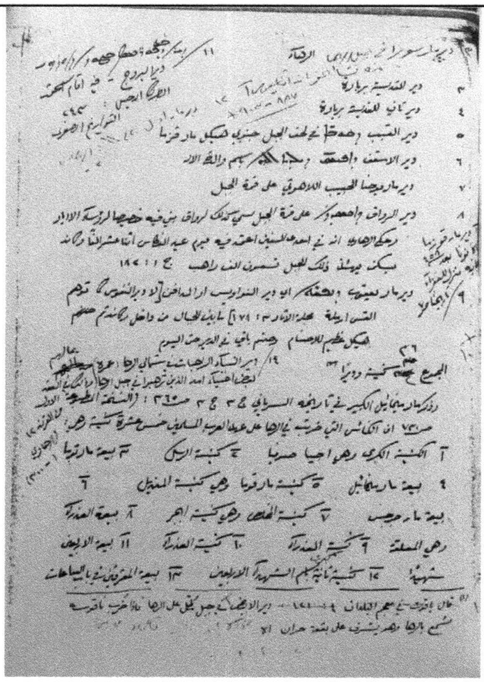

Figure 3.5: Page 327 of Barsoum's Diocese Manuscript related to the Diocese of Edessa (Urhoy)

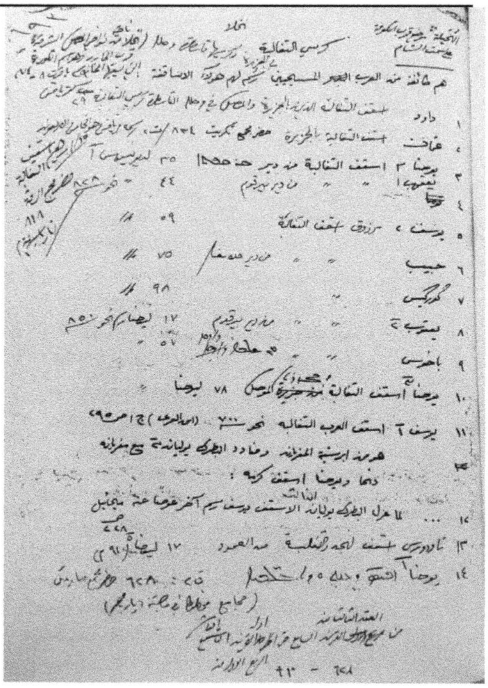

Figure 3.6: Page 304 of Barsoum's Diocese of Mar-Matti Monastery

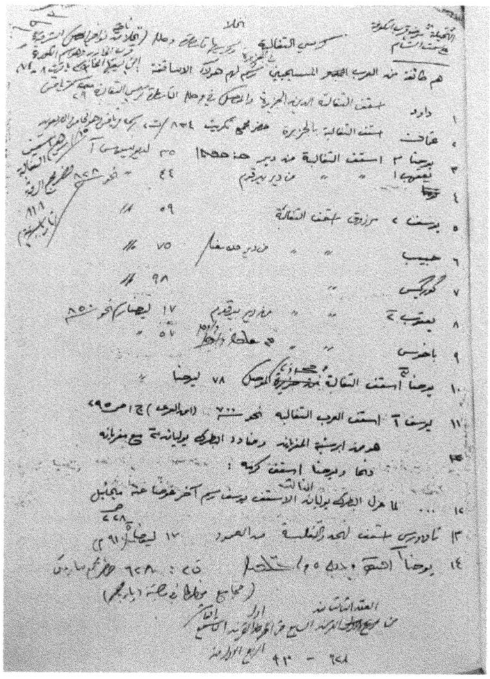

Figure 3.7: Page 193 of Barsoum's Manuscript Related to the Diocese of Taghlib.

A LOOK AT ONE OF THE FIRST ARMENIAN PLAYS IN IRAN

DUMAN RIYAZI
UNIVERSITY OF TORONTO

Undoubtedly, the culture of the "Armenian Iranians" can be counted among the most important in the history of Iran—a culture that, for all its differences and similarities, was able to create important integrations and influences in Iran. A clear example of such integrations is to be found in cultural and artistic influences. Especially in the performing arts.

The Armenians who moved to Iran during the Safavid era soon began to establish their own community, and it was not until years later that theatrical performances were gradually introduced into their own communities.

Armenian theater of Iran bears great influence of the Armenian theater of the Caucasus. Thinkers and all local artists tried to keep Armenian theater culture alive in Iran. In the meantime, and quite apart from the dramatic and literary books brought to Iran mainly by travelers and merchants from the East and West, the cultural and artistic relations of Iranian Armenians with Tbilisi, Baku and Yerevan became more and more colorful.

Perhaps it can be said that these Armenian communities were one of the most important factors in actualizing Iranian drama during the Qajar period. In this article, we will try to present and review one of the first Armenian drama documents of Iran during the Qajar period.

Around 1603, when Armenia was under the rule of the powerful and destructive Ottomans, the Shah of Iran inevitably decided to evacuate the community. At the time, perhaps few suspected that this migration would lead to bilateral cultural integration, but gradually this matter took shape in Jolfa. It is no exaggeration to call New Jolfa,[1] with its more than four hundred years of history, one of the most important cultural centers of Armenians in Iran and the Middle East. With more than 120 years of social and cultural activity, it can be said that New Jolfa is one of the oldest theatrical centers of the Armenian diaspora.

With the beginning of a new life in a new culture, the cultural and artistic activities of Armenians also began. In the intervening period, the performing arts were one of the most important expressions of this society, whose activities, besides their traditional and local customs, went a step further and opened the community's eyes to the famous Western texts. Merchants and travelers who traveled to other countries for various reasons had a cultural view of their society from the very beginning; this led these people to bring noble literary texts to Iran. Among such books are valuable and exquisite works of Schiller and Shakespeare. And other famous authors of the world can also be seen.[2]

There are different opinions about the date of the beginning of Jolfa Theater. Each of these researchers in the field of history and theater espouses distinct opinions, but most of them see the beginning of the New Jolfa Theater occurring between 1886-1888. The most important point in this field, however, is the consensus of most of those theorizing about a theater performance. It is the latter that we will discuss in this article.

In the library and archives of the Vank[3] there are two important documents that contain very important information about this piece.

Document number one.

Vank Church Library, Isfahan, Iran

The translation as follows:

Kechoe's Fig[4]

Fars Vaudeville[5]
In a curtain
The work of Emin Ter Grigorian
second edition
Printed House of Emil Ter Grigorian 1894

Document number two

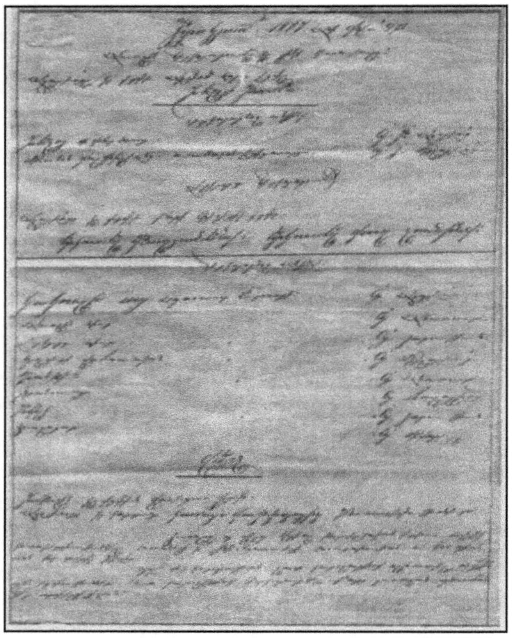

www.abcarians.com

The translation is as follows:

9 February 1887 Program
The first piece will be as follows
Mr. Aghaians will sing the Armenian song of Aragats[6]
Kechoe's Fig

Performers:
Khacho Khechoe (an ignorant servant)
Mr. Aghayans Aghaians.
Monon Kalpichians (educated young man)
Mr. Mirzayans Mirzaians.

Second part,
Mr. Aghaians will sing a beautiful and good song.[7]

We are Both Hungry, We are Both Penniless

Actors

Kakoli Vai (guest house servant)	Mr. Aghaians
The first guest	Mr. Asdevadzador
The second guest	Mr. Haroutiuon
Marketers from Istanbul	Mr. Mirzaians
Dante	Mr. Master
Francois	Mr. Jalalian
Medic	Mr. Haroutioun
Sofleur (reminder of the text of the play)	Mr. Michael

End

The group sings the song of the City of Van[8] together.

Mr. Aghaians reads poetry by Gamar Katipa.[9]

We hope that these two short comic performances will please you, dear audience, and that you will be satisfied with our small stage.

We have tried our best to show our national jeremiad,[10] but various factors have prevented us from doing so.

The play *Khechoe's Fig*, along with another show titled *We are Both Hungry, We are Both Penniless*, is one of the first performances of the Armenian community in Iran which was first performed in Rasht[11] and then in Jolfa, Isfahan.

These two playas are ready to be performed on February 9, 1887, in Jolfa, Isfahan, and at Simon's house by Beglar Aghaians and Hovsep Mirzaians. This house, which is in the form of a garden house, was originally owned by a person named Simon, and was later bought by the Vank Church.

Servant and Master Plays have a long history in the important theatre cultures of the world, and from *the Commedia dell'arte* to the Persian Takht Hozei,[12] there are always two social classes that comprise the two main poles of this form of play, the lower class and the upper class of society.

The servant always comes from the lower class of society and usually has his wits about him and his cleverness, and on the other side there is a master who is either old and stingy or educated. The confrontation of these two groups in the scene of the verbal comedy creates a situation that is very attractive to the audience. But apart from this stage attraction, there is one very important point in this performance (*Khechoe's Fig*), and that is that there are only two actors in this play, which makes it very difficult for the actors and requires a very high art of performance.

Another point is the awareness of the creators of this show of the Iranian form and the Western possibility of this show's genre, which of course with our knowledge about the cultural relations of Iranian Armenians can lead to a very striking composition.

AN ANALYTICAL LOOK

In both exhibitions appear the names of two prominent figures, Beglar Aghaians and Hovsep Mirzaians, who founded and organized the core of the theater first in Rasht (1884) and then in New Jolfa, Isfahan (1887).

Hovsep Mirzaians is a famous and well-known figure in the Armenian community of Iran, but Beglar Aghaians was probably a friend of taste and opinion of his, who worked together with him to create a role in the field of theatrical art. At that time, Mirzaians was a nineteen-year-old educated young man with modernist and intellectual thoughts who should have helped a person like Beglar Aghaians in this sacred matter. Unfortunately, there is little information about the life and personality of Aghaians. We only know that he was from Karabakh,[13] and that he lived in

Tabriz and traveled to Isfahan and Shiraz in the late nineteenth century, studying the art of photography.[14]

In document number one, the title page of a play published in 1894, we are given most of the basic information about this play, including the title of the play and the author of the work, but the mention of one item may indicate important information, and that is the one immediately below: the name of the play refers to the Tatar genre that was popular in the United States of America and Canada from 1880 to 1930. According to the application of this kind of genre to this piece, there are two situations. First, the creator of the work created this piece with full knowledge of this type of drama, which is very commendable. Considering that in vaudeville most shows are performed episodically, but with different themes and completely separate from each other, *Khechoe's Fig* was perhaps a part of episodic plays performed at different times and close to each other.

On the other hand, we can refer to the publications that published this play later and to the fact that even if the publisher attributed the play to this genre, it can be said that the play definitely had four mentioned editions of this genre. Which the publisher mentioned.

A CHRONOLOGICAL LOOK

Tigran Abkarian,15 who was the secretary of the New Jolfa National Theater Association in different years and organized performances for children, writes in his book *New Jolfa National Theater (1888-1913)* that the activity of the New Jolfaian Theater began with the performance of *Khechoe's Fig* in 1888. He knows this, but a few years later, in an article published in the *Armenian Yearbook of Iran*, and titled "Theater," he pushes back the date to 1886. Aram Yeremian,16 among other experts in the field of literature and culture, considered the year to be 1888. This is based on the book of Abkarian and the history of the anniversary of the founding of the theater of works on the cultural life of New Jolfa, attributes the beginning of the theater activity to the year 1886 in his book *The Theater of New Jolfa (1886-1986)*.

Nikit Mirzaians, one of the researchers and thinkers of the New Jolfa, in an article on the occasion of the 125th anniversary of the New Jolfa Theater, has a different opinion. According to document number two, he believes that on February 9, 1887, two short comedies, *Khechoe's Fig*, and *We are Both Hungry, We are Both Penniless*, were performed. The interesting thing about Nikit Mirzaians is that he is the grandson of Mr. Mirzaians, who plays the role of an educated young man in this play.

CONCLUSION

As it has been shown, with the beginning of a new life in a new geography and the expansion of relations with the East and the West, the way to the Western theater was opened to the Armenian communities. The existence of famous and well-known theater books and plays brought to Iran (its Armenian communities) over many years by Armenian merchants and travelers is a proof of this.

In this article, an attempt has been made to provide an accurate translation of two documents from the *Khechoe's Fig* exhibit.

Apart from mentioning the exact date when this show was performed, one can take a very detailed and scholarly look at the category of the show in the society of that time. Armenians pointed out an allegorical view that over time led to the integration and promotion of Armenian theatre culture outside Iran and they can perhaps becalled one of the main poles of the actualization of Iranian drama in the Qajar period.

NOTES

[1] An ancient Armenian region built during the Safavid period in the city of Isfahan near the Zayandeh Rood. The name New Jolfa comes from the name of the city of Jolfa on the Northern bank of the Aras River which is considered part of a region called Nakhchevan, whose inhabitants are mainly Armenians. The Armenians of New Jolfa were resettled to Isfahan in 1605 during the reign of Shah Abbas I of the Safavids.

[2] One of the best Shakespearean performers was Hovhannes Khan Masehian (1864-1931), nicknamed Mosaed al-Sultaneh, Armenian writer and diplomat, first independent minister of Iran in Japan, Germany and Great Britain, and the Armenian representative in the sixth legislature of the National Assembly.

[3] This is the name of a church in the Jolfa district of Isfahan, built during the time of Shah Abbas II. Vank means monastery in Armenian. The church and the adjacent building formed the religious and social center of the Armenians of Isfahan, southern Iran, and at the time referred to in this article; it was also the religious center of the Armenians in India.

[4] Khechoe is a name and in Armenian it is an abbreviation of the name Khachatur.

[5] A comic kind of theatre, which originated in France at the end of the nineteenth century and later spread to Canada and the United States of America.

[6] **Արագած**. This refers to a song about a mountain called Aragats in Armenia, which has five peaks.

[7]A reference to two important and nostalgic Armenian songs.

[8] There are several songs about Van, but the important thing about these songs is that they mention the Armenians of Van city, which is one of the most important Armenian cities in Western Armenia.

[9] Gamar Katipa, a literary group in Moscow (1854), whose founders were Raphael Patkanian, Mnatsakan Teymurian and George Kananian. This name is derived from the initials of the founders' first and last names along with the vowel "a." Their goal was to develop the Armenian literary language, which at that time was changing from its ancient form (so that it could be understood by the general public), to promote and instill a love of study in the Armenian communities, and to instill national consciousness in the minds of Armenians.

[10] This may refer to the plight of Armenians in Armenia under the Ottoman rule or the rule of the Russian Empire.

[11] Nikit Mirzaians, in his article published in *Peyman Cultural Quarterly* 57, believes that these two plays were performed for the first time on January 28, 1884 in Rasht (City in North of Iran).

[12] The principal kind of Persian comedy.

[13] A geographical region in eastern Armenia and southwestern Azerbaijan.

[14] Nikit Mirzaians, *Peyman Cultural Quarterly* No. 57, Tehran 2011.

[15] (1877-1950) philologist, orator, from Julfa Isfahan.

[16] (1898-1972) writer, art theorist, and graduated from Vienna University of History.

CALENDAR, POPULAR MEDICAL PRESCRIPTIONS AND TREATMENTS, AND THE ZODIAC CIRCLE

AMIR HARRAK
UNIVERSITY OF TORONTO

Syriac Christianity, as other cultures in antiquity (and modern times), was interested, not to say fascinated, by astrology, a secular literature par excellence. There are many manuscripts that named the constellations, including Aries, Taurus, Cancer, Libra, Sagittarius, Capricorn, and Pisces. The reason behind the Zodiac is partially liturgical. For example:

> "October: its days are 31; its day hours are 11; its night hours are 13; on the 23rd of it, the sun enters the sign of the scorpion; its moon is born in the first hours of the day, and it has 30 days. On the 7th of it is the feast of Mār Sergius and Bacchus, and on the 15th in it is the feast of Mār Asiā the Sage and of Mār Ešaʿiā of Aleppo."

Needless to say, other pieces of information are included in the Zodiac, for example, there would be lack of wheat and barley if the beginning of October occurs on Wednesday!

MANUSCRIPT 41404

The Iraqi Department of Antiquities and Heritage owns a collection of Syriac manuscripts probably still stored in the Iraqi Centre of Manuscripts located in Baghdad, not far from the Iraqi Museum. I studied this Syriac collection in 1997, while I was working on Syriac epigraphy, and eventually published their 2011 catalogue in Leuven, in the *CSCO Subsidia* 126.[1]

The collection of diverse manuscripts was established in 1924 at the Iraq Museum and the Syriac collection of some 43 items was donated by former directors of the Iraq Museum and Library, including Gorgīs ʿAwwād (d. 1992), and especially the Carmelite monk Anistas Mārī al-Kirmilī (d. 1947). The Carmelite Library had previously donated some 6000 books, as well as 1335 manuscripts, to the Iraq Museum. It is quite possible that this important collection of manuscripts included the afore-mentioned Syriac codices.

Among the Syriac manuscripts, in Garshuni (Arabic written with Syriac script), identified under the number 41404, is dated probably to 19th century. It is about astrology and even the Zodiac circle is represented therein. In Syriac the Zodiac is called ܡܠܘܫܐ (*malwōšō*) and the same in Jewish Aramaic (מַלְוָשָׁא).[2] The manuscript has a Syriac title in folio 1, although the rest is in Garshuni, but water darkened some of the early folios. The script is unvocalized Syriac, and thus it must have been produced by the Syriac Orthodox community most probably in Mosul—some words are known only in this city (see below). The manuscript is layout has one column made of 12 lines each, and the total of its folios is fifty-one. It measures 10.5 × 7.5 cm, whick not too voluminous. The is scribed on paper and has a cardboard cover. It is not complete and even partially damaged by humidity.

THE CODEX

The codex is a calendar with astronomical[3] and meteorological observations, the wheel of the zodiac, with advice related to popular medicine and hygiene.[4] It seems to draw on medieval Greek sources translated into Syriac and Arabic during the Abbasid period. Hubayš, the nephew of the famous translator Ḥunayn ibn-Isḥāq, is credited with a treatise on popular medicine and hygiene.[5]

A popular Syriac work entitled ܟܬܒܐ ܕܣܡ̈ܡܢܐ "Book of remedies"[6] also includes a note on the days of the month of *Tammūz* (July), calendar of lunar (Islamic) months, the Book of Fate and the influence of the latter on sickness and health, etc.[7]

The present codex is understandably anonymous and undated, as the information is general. The Dominican Father Vosté[8] published a note on dates reported by the present codex.[9] This was a popular treatise judging from the many manuscripts bearing either title.[10]

TOPICS

The topics of the present codex features various subjects as follows:

- Medical: 3 cases
- Remedy for Burns: 1 case
- Calendar: 2 cases
- Eclipse: 1 one case
- Intercourse: 2 cases
- Pregnancy: 1 case

The categorization of cases is thematic, to facilitate reading them:

POPULAR MEDICINE

Scientific medicine was probably not very advanced in Iraq in 1924, and in any case, until recently, there was in the city Mosul (north of the country) and elsewhere in Iraq *sūq al-'aṭṭārīn* "Market of Spices," some of its contents used to remedy certain medical cases. This explains why the codex under study uses spices, as was the case for thousands of years in the Land between the Rivers."

THE CODEX TITLE

Folio 1 may have the following title: ܡܛܠ ܟܪ̈ܝܗܐ ܘܡܛܠ ܒܪܘܣܐ ܘܡܛܠܛ̣![1] ܡܕܡ ܕܐܒܕ "For the sick, for the sweating, and for! the (sickness?) that perishes (wastes away)." The third Syriac word at the end must be ܘܡܛܠ instead of the erroneous ܘܡܛܠܛ. The triple dots under *lōmad* and *ṭēt* may refer to the faulty spelling. The word "sick" justified the inclusion of this item in the context of medical treatment.

The Codex is not limited to sicknesses, as the possible title claims, but to other subjects, including predictions proclaimed by the Zodiac, and even ink making!

The title of **Folio 1v** continues the partial medical treatise, as it differentiates between *ġālib* "the victorious" and *maġlūb* "the defeated." Does this mean the *ġālib* is the winner (or healed one) and the *maġlūb* is the fallen sick?

ܐܝܨ̇ܐ ܢܟܬܒ ܟܬܐܒܐܬ ܗܘܝ //
ܐܠܓ̇ܐܠܒ ܘܐܠܡܓ̇ܠܘܒ

"We also write texts: the victorious and the defeated one."

The following item is curious: if someone falls sick on Sunday, his sickness becomes serious. Worst, if the person does not die, his sickness becomes even more serious. Is it because Sunday is a holy day in Christianity? Then, how could that sickness become so serious to the point of death on that holy day?

Folio 5r

ܢܟܬܘܒ ܒܐܒ ܦܣܩܢܝܬܐ ܐܠܡܪܥ ܡܢ
ܡܪܥ ܝܘܡ ܐܠܐܚܕ. ܝܡܪܥ // ܡܪܥ
ܫܕܝܕ ܘܝܫܪܦ ܥܠ ܐܠܡܘܬ // ܦܐܢ ܠܡ
ܝܡܘܬ ܐܠܐ ܣܒܥܬ ܐܝܐܡ ܝܨܝܪ.
[6FOb] ܡܪܥܗ (...)

"We are writing a chapter (made of) deadly sickness. He who becomes sick on Sunday, he would fall into a heavy sickness to the point of death. If he would not die after seven days, his sickness grows even more severe (…)."

The term ܦܣܩܢܝܬܐ, singular ܦܣܩ "cut off," means "determination (or condition) of death," or "deadly (disease)," in both Syriac and Jewish Aramaic.[11] Arabic قَطَعَ "cut off" is related to Syriac ܦܣܩܢܝܬܐ, in the phrase قطع أمل الحياة "he cut off the hope for life." ܠܡ ܝܡܘܬ is colloquial for classical ܠܡ ܝܡܬ.

In **Folio 8r**, the title is mostly effaced, but the content of the chapter discusses a remedy involving ܥܪܩ ܐܠܣܘܣ "licorice," hence a vegetal drink. Until recently, at least in the north of Iraq, liquid licorice, stored inside skin of animals, is sold by itinerant sellers. The latter plays musical sounds with two metal recipients to attract the attention of possible buyers of licorice. Probably this was done throughout Mesopotamian history, and in any case, drinking fresh licorice in the hot summer, is indeed refreshing!

BURNS

It is clear from the context that the aforementioned recipe is meant to remedy burns. Many nominal and verbal forms indicate that the codex was produced in Mosul, through colloquial imperatives: *jīb* "bring," *k̲ed̲* "take!" for *k̲ud̲; wa-dhen* for *wa-dhun* (spelled elsewhere in the text *'udhun*) "anoint!" and *uk̲luṭ* "mix!" (for *kluṭ*) and especially the term *malīḥ* "well" (from *milḥ* "salt," i.e. "salted"!), and the term *kāġad* "paper." Such terms are still used in Mosul, where the letter /r/ is systematically changed to /*ġ*/.[12]

Folio 9r at the bottom contains a treatment for burns:

ܨܦܬ! ܕܘܐ ܐܠܚܪܩ ܓܝܒ ܟܐܓܕ ܟܕ.
ܘܐܚܪܩܗܡ ܘܒܥܕ ܬܪܐܒܗܡ ܘܕܗܢܗ ܣܘܝ
ܘܟܠܛܗܡ ܒܐܠܕܗܢ ܘܐܟܠܛܗܡ ܡܠܝܚ
ܘܐܕܗܢܗ ܥܠܝ ܐܠܚܪܩ

"Recipe for remedy for burns: bring papers and burn them, then take their ashes and put them in animal oil and mix them together well. Then apply on the burn."

F9r and **F31v**: The first word is to be read is ܘܨܦܗ "recipe," instead of the original ܨܦܗ, which means "adjective."

The term *māliḥ*, lit. "salty," is here in the sense of "good." This term is used in Mosul, which means that the codex was done in this city.

ASTROLOGICAL CALENDARS

The Zodiac circle is partially damaged in the codex, but examining it *in situ*, the traces of central ܫܡܫ could be seen:

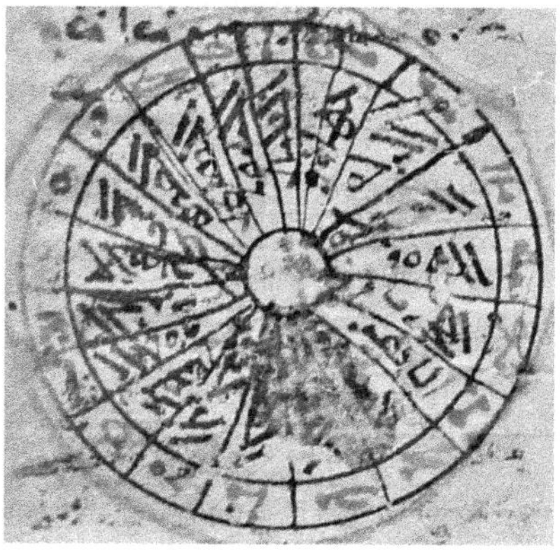

The Zodiac in Manuscript (Photo© A. Harrak)

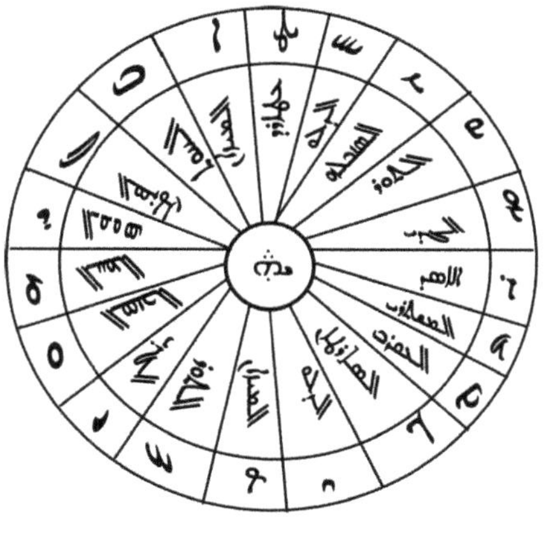

Drawing of a Syriac Zodiac

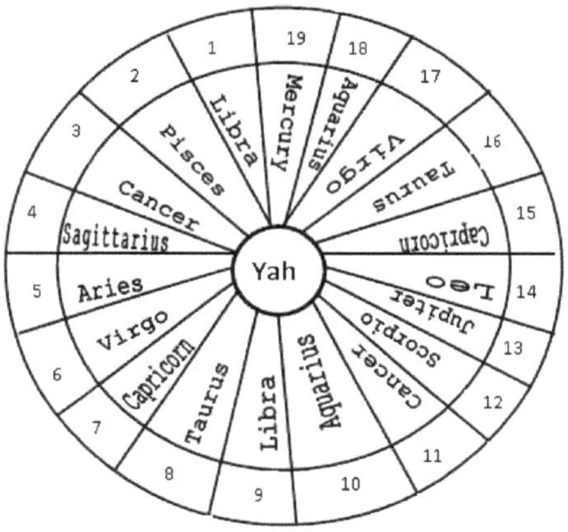

English Rendering of the Zodiac

The history of the Zodiac, whether Babylonian or Greek, is known as it relates to agriculture and the raising of domestic animals—ancient and modern practices known nowadays internationally.[13] The terms in the current Zodiac are all in Arabic, including animals like *ṯawr* "Taurus" (Syriac ܬܘܪܐ) and *ḥūt* "Pisces" (Syriac ܢܘܢܐ); constellations like *'uṭārid* "Mercury" (Syriac ܢܒܘ) and *mīzān* "Libra" (Syriac ܡܣܐܬܐ); agricultural terms like *sunbul* "wheat" (Syriac ܚܛܬܐ).[14] This means that the author got his information from Arab sources not Syriac.[15] When the sun passes through these symbols, dates are provided.

The current Zodiac is probably of Greek origin, but it is produced by Christians given the fact that the Biblical name of God Yah(we) (=Yahve) is placed in the centre. Yah is found in many manuscripts, especially in the form ܘܠܝܗ ܫܘܒܚܐ "and to Yah(we) the glory!"[16] The three dots above Yah refers to the Trinity. The Zodiac circle is given above, with an English rendering to facilitate recognition of astronomical terms.

F10v: The Zodiac circle, drawn with the names of each symbol, and what follows are predictions of the future:

ܘܐܢ ܟܐܢ ܬܫܪܝܢ ܐܠܐܘܠ ܝܘܡ ܐܠܐܪܒܥܐ ܝܟܘܢ ܢܩܨ ܦܝ
ܐܠܚܢܛܗ ܘܐܠܫܥܝܪ ܘܒܐܩܝ ܐܠܙܪܘܥܐܬ [...]

"If *First Tišrīn* (October) falls on *'Arba'ā'* (a Wednesday), there would be want of wheat, barley and the rest of the seeds [...]."

F17-18: is mostly missing.

F24r: Between two simplistic arabesques, a Garshuni text talks about Christian feast days, another indication that this Zodiac is of Christian origin:

F25v: contains information about each month:

ܬܫܪܝܢ ܐܠܐܘܠ ܐܝܐܡܗ ܟܐ̄ ܣܐܥܐܬ ܢܗܐܪܗ ܝܐ̄
ܘܣܐܥܐܬ ܠܝܠܗ ܝܓ̄ ܘܦܝ ܟܓ̄ ܡܢܗ ܬܕܟܠ
ܐܠܫܡܣ ܦܝ ܒܪܓ ܐܠܥܩܪܒ ܘܩܡܪܗ ܝܘܠܕ
ܦܝ ܐܘܠ ܣܐܥܐܬ ܡܢ ܐܠܢܗܐܪ ܘܗܘ ܠ̄ ܝܘܡ
ܘܦܝ ܙ̄ ܡܢܗ ܥܝܕ ܡܪܝ ܣܪܓܝܣ ܘܒܐܟܘܣ
ܘܦܝ ܝܗ̄ ܡܢܗ ܥܝܕ ܡܪܝ ܐܣܝܐ ܐܠܚܟܝܡ ܘܡܐܪ
ܐܫܥܝܐ ܐܠܚܠܒܝ

"*First Tišrīn* (October): its days are 31; its day hours are 11; its night hours are 13; on the 23rd of it, the sun enters the sign of the Scorpion; its moon is born in the first hours of the day, and it has 30 days. On the 7th of it is the feast of Mār Sergius and Bacchus, and on the 15th in it is the feast of Mār Asiā the Sage and of Mār Eša'iā of Aleppo."

The third line before the end the signs ܙ̈ must be just one sign: ܙ "seven." That the compiler was a Syriac Orthodox man is beyond doubt not only on account of the Serto script, but also because of the feasts included in the calendar of the Syriac Orthodox (and Catholic) Church. The feast of Sts. Sergius and Bacchus indeed falls on October 7, and that of Mār Asiā and of Mār Ešaʿiā of Aleppo, altogether, occurs on October 15.[17] These feast dates agree with the Zodiac data, including even the names of the holy personalities.

INK MAKING

Writing was created by the Sumerians in the south of Mesopotamia in cuneiform shapes, and scribes wrote on clay, readily available in Mesopotamia. Their Syriac counterparts used ink, which must also be of Mesopotamian origin—during the Seleucid period, clay tablets partially bear black ink writings.

> **F31v** ܐܝܒܐ ܨܦܗ̈! ܚܒܪ ܠܘܢ ܐܠܓܣܡ "Also a recipe (to make) ink of the colour of the body."

Read ܘܨܦܗ "recipe" instead of ܨܦܗ̈ "adjective," as also indicated above. The ink colour "of the body" must be rather light! No information is given on how to make ink in gold colour, as the following description tells:

> **F33v** ܥܡܠ ܚܒܪ ܕܗܒܝ "The making of golden ink."

The Syriac (and Arabic) term ܕܗܒܝ is an adjective describing the ink.

ECLIPSES

The term eclipse, of Greek origin (ἔκλειψις), means "the darkening of a heavenly body." It happens when a body hides the sun completely or partially. The results of eclipses in the month of *Muḥarram* suggests that the current writer relied on Arabic sources for prediction, for *Muḥarram* is the beginning of the Islamic year. How fertility results if the eclipse happened in the beginning of this Muslim month is difficult to imagine! Eclipses last short times.

> **F38v** ܢܘܥ ܦܝ ܟܣܘܦ ܐܠܫܡܣ ܦܝ
> ܫܗܘܪ ܐܠܥܪܒܝܗ: ܐܕܐ ܐܢܟܣܦܬ ܦܝ ܫܗܪ
> ܡܚܪܡ ܬܟܘܢ ܣܢܗ ܡܟܨܒܗ [...]
>
> "One kind of a solar eclipse in the Arab months: If the eclipse occurs in the month of *Muḥarram*, the year would be fertile [...]."

The phrase "Arab month" means that the writer quoted an Arabic source. In fact, eclipses occur for a short time so that they have no effect on agriculture.

Interestingly, the Chronicle of Zuqnīn, written in 776 AD, reported an eclipse that may have lasted one year (!).[18] In fact, the second letter of the word for "year" is darkened and so it is not known if it is ܫܢܬܐ "year" or ܫܥܬܐ "hour"! The latter word is more credible. In another passage, the Chronicler stated: "In the month of First *Tešrīn* (October) of this year (AD 499-50), on the twenty-third, a Saturday, at the rising of the sun, its light (sun) was taken away, and its radiant disk looked like silver. It did not have visible rays and our eyes stare could easily and without hindrance at it, for it had no brilliance, brightness, or rays to prevent those who would gaze at it. Just as it is easy for us to look at the moon, so was it easy when we looked at it. It remained likewise until toward the eighth hour." In this case, the eclipse lasted short times as the Chronicler credibly declared.

> **F40v** ܢܘܥ ܐܚܪ ܦܝ ܟܣܘܦܗܐ ܚܐܠܝܢ
> ܐܠܒܪܘܓ
>
> "Another kind of its eclipse while in one of the [Zodiac] signs."

SEXUAL INTERCOURSE

Impotence is a problem facing many men, even in our time, but there is yet a popular recipe to remedy it, but the issue is how to get all these ingredients from the market? Probably one could obtain them from *sūq al-ʿaṭṭārīn* "Market of Spices," mentioned above:

F43v ܕܘܐ ܠܓܒܪ ܠܐ ܡܫܟܚܝܢ ܠܓܡܥܐ ܣܒ
ܟܡܘܢ ܟܪܡܐܢܝ ܘܟܪܘܝܐ ܘܚܪܕܠ ܘܒܪܙ ܓܪܓܝܪ
ܘܡܠܚ ܗܢܕܝ ܡܢ ܟܠ ܐܚܕ ܕܪܗܡ ܘܡܚܠܛ
ܦܫ ܒܚܠܬ ܒܝܥܬܗ ܘܡܫܘܦ ܘܡܫܬܐ ܒܬܪܗ
ܢܒܝܕ ܥܬܝܩ

"Medicine for impotent men: Take one *dirhem* of each of the following: Kerman cumin, caraway, mustard, garden rocket's seeds, and Indian salt. Then crush and mix with the white of one egg. After (taking the mixture), drink old wine."

Kermani is the gentilic of Kerman, a city in Iran, and Indian salt can be easily imported from that country. Trade relation with India is attested in ancient Mesopotamian history from the distant past. Another recipe useful not only for intercourse but also for backache and knee pain. It goes without saying, the man who suffers these pains cannot have intercourse!

F43r ܕܘܐ ܡܪܒܐ ܦܫ ܠܫܘܗܘܬܐ ܦܫ ܠܓܡܥܐ
ܘܡܥܕܪ ܡܢ ܟܐܒ ܠܚܨܐ ܘܠܒܘܪܟܐ܀ ܣܒ
ܟܡܘܢ ܘܟܘܪܟܡܐ ܘܡܚܘܛ ܒܕܒܫܐ ܡܢܩܝܐ
ܠܓܥܘܪܐ ܘܣܒ ܡܢܗ ܡܟܝܠܬ ܠܒܠܘܛܐ ܟܠ
ܝܘܡ ܠܬܠܬܐ ܝܘܡܝܢ ܒܡܝܐ [ܩܪ]ܝܪܐ ܘܡܫܬܐ ܟܣܐ
ܚܕ ܢܒܝܕ ܝܬܝܪ

"Medicine which increases libido and is also useful for backache and knee pain. Take cumin and saffron and mix with foamless honey. Take as much as the volume of a gallnut every day for three days in [co]ld water, and drink a glass of useful wine thereafter."

Advice for Pregnant Women

Another recipe for pregnant women consisting of "oral powder" that chase away winds and bad desire.

F44v ܣܦܘܦ ܠܒܛܢܬܐ ܠܫܘܐܠܐ ܕܦܘܡ
ܠܦܘܡ ܠܐܪܘܚܐ ܘܡܟܠܐ ܠܫܘܗܘܬܐ ܠܒܝܫܬܐ
ܣܒ ܟܡܘܢ ܟܪܡܐܢܝ ܘܢܒܛܝ ܘܒܪܙ ܠܟܪܦܣ
ܘܐܢܝܣܘܢ ܡܢ ܟܠ ܚܕ ܚܡܫܐ ܕܪܗܡ. ܙܪܢܒܕ
ܕܪܗܡܝܢ. ܩܪܢܦܠ ܕܪܗܡ ܫܘܫܡܐ ܓܪܝ ܫܒܥܐ
ܫܒܥܐ ܕܪܗܡ. ܚܕ ܠܓܡܥܐ ܢܫܬܐ
ܘܠܡܬܒܪ ܡܢܗ ܕܪܗܡܝܢ ܒܡܝܐ ܩܪܝܪܐ܀܀

"Oral powder for pregnant women for the expulsion of winds and preventing bad desire. Take Kerman cumin, Nabatean cumin, celery seeds, anis, five *dirhems* of each, of zranbad [zingiber zerumbet] two *dirhems*, of cloves one *dirhem*, and of unhulled sesame seven *dirhems*, all crushed fine. Drink two *dirhems* with cold water (at a time)."

The measurement of 1 *dirhem* equals 3.186 gm. Nabatean cumin is imported from Syria by the *ʿaṭṭārūn* "spice importers" and is therefore easily accessible.

Conclusion

The Zodiac signs and horoscopes are the most popular worldwide, as some people rely on them for their livelihood and fates. Manuscripts comprising remedies and medicinal recipes abound in most catalogues of Syriac (and Arabic) manuscripts and used by doctors and patients throughout the ages. They are also attested in manuscripts as in BM Add. 14.478[19] and even in private homes as in Qaraqōš.[20] Moreover, a bronze censer at the Iraq Museum (no. 11243/1)[21] has several registers, the third one depicts Sagittarius (9th sign), Leo (5th sign), and Aries the ram (1st sign). Sagittarius also figures at the bottom of the incense burner.

NOTES

[1] A. Harrak, *Catalogue of Syriac and Garshuni Manuscripts: Manuscripts Owned by the Iraqi Department of Antiquities and Heritage* CSCO 639 Subsidia 126 (Leuven, 108-112). §41404 is expanded in the current article based on further notes available to the author.

[2] Michael Sokoloff, *A Dictionary of Jewish Babylonian Aramaic of the Talmudic and Geonic Periods* (Ramat-Gan: Bar Ilan University Press (and) Baltimore, Maryland: The Johns Hopkins University Press, 2002), 677.

[3] For liturgical purposes see Sánchez et als., *Catalogue des manuscrits conservés dans la bibliothèque de l'archevêché grec-catholique d'Alep (Syrie)* (Wiesbaden: Reichert, 2003), 189 §438: في معرفه اخراج الفصح المقدس وفصح الناموس ومعرفه اوايل الشهور واشيا اخر .....

[4] On astronomy see Paṭros Ḥaddād & Jāk Isḥāq, *Al-maḵṭūṭāt al-suryāniyya w-al-'Arabiyya* I: *Al-maḵṭūṭāt al-suryāniyya* (Baghdad, 1988), §78: 6, §978.

[5] Graf, *Geschichte der Christlichen Arabischen* Literatur, 2:113-114.

[6] On this popular genre see E. A. Wallis Budge, *The Book of Medicines: Ancient Syrian Anatomy, Pathology and Therapeutics* (London, UK, New York: Kegan Paul, 2002). See also Ḥaddād-Isḥāq, *Al-maḵṭūṭāt al-suryāniyya*, §942, §943, §945, §947, §948, etc. On medication see in the same source: §511:9, §572:3, §637:6, §939, §940, §942, §943, §946:12, §955:2.

[7] See on such item in Vosté, *Notre-Dame*, §327=Ḥaddād-Isḥāq, *Al-maḵṭūṭāt al-suryāniyya*, 1: §939.

[8] Ibid.

[9] On the genre see Budge, *The Book of Medicines: Ancient Syrian Anatomy, Pathology and Therapeutics.*

[10] Paṭros Ḥaddād & Jāk Isḥāq, *Al-maḵṭūṭāt al-suryāniyya,* 1:939=Addai Scher, "Notice…," 153= Vosté, *Notre-Dame,* 327—Scher tends to think that this Book is of Ḥunain ibn Isḥāq. For other occurrences of this and related manuscripts see Ḥaddād-Isḥāq, *Al-maḵṭūṭāt al-suryāniyya,* I: §942, §943, §945, §946, §947, §948.

[11] Abbātī (=Abbé) Jubrā'īl al-Qardāḥī, *Al-Lubāb: Qāmūṣ Suriānī 'Arabī* (Aleppo: Syriac Patrimony, 1994), 1013. The same meaning is attested in Judaism (cut off, kill); see Sokoloff, *A Dictionary of Jewish Babylonian Aramaic,* 1008.

[12] *Waraq* must derive from YRQ "yellow," when leaves of trees turn to this colour in Autumn. It is a well-known fact that papers used to be made out of trees.

[13] A Persian treatise is called رسالة في علم الفلك "Letter on the Science of Astronomy" by Ḥasan ibn Muḥammad al-Qummī (died in H 750 = AD 1349)—is it astronomy or astronomy?; see Sánchez et als., *Catalogue des manuscrits,* 109 §242; كتاب في بيان الهيئة "Book of the Compendium of the Structure," by Maḥmūd al-Jaġmānī, *Ibid*, p. 144-5 §329.

[14] More of Syriac symbols: ܓܕܝܐ = Capricorn; ܕܠܝܐ = Aquarius; ܣܪܛܢܐ = Cancer; ܥܩܪܒܐ = Scorpio; ܥܛܪܕ, (planet); Mercury (planet); ܐܪܝܐ = Leo; ܐܪܝܣ = Aries.

[15] On astrology see Ḥaddād & Isḥāq, *Al-maḵṭūṭāt al-suryāniyya,* 1: §954 (ملاحظات فلكية). This manuscript provides information on what is permissible and not permissible food in very month of the year. There is no date to this incomplete manuscript.

[16] See W. Wright, *Catalogue of Syriac Manuscripts in the British Museum* I (London: British Museum, 1870), 95. The manuscript containing the Letters of Paul dates to Seleucid 1823 (=AD 1512). There are many manuscripts that contains this expression.

[17] *Šlāwōṯō d-yawmōṯō šḥīmē d-šabṯō* [Prayers for the Simple Days of the Week] (Charfeh: Imprimerie Patriarcale, 1996), 711-712. The Syriac Catholic and Orthodox Churches share the same calendric schedules.

[18] A. Harrak, *The Chronicle of Zuqnīn Partss I and II: from the Creation to the Year 506/7 AD* (Piscataway: Gorgias Press, 2017), 184.

[19] Jules Leroy, *Les Manuscrits Syriaques à Peintures* II (Paris, Librairie Orientaliste Paul Geuthner, 1964), 159 fig. 1; vol. I, 419-420 (discussion).

[20] A. Harrak, *Syriac and Garshuni Inscriptions of Iraq* (Paris: Académie des Inscriptions et Lettres, 2010), AD.08.02.

[21] A. Harrak, "The Incense Burner of Takrit;" *Eastern Christian Art* 3 (2006), pp. 47-52.

THE PAGE LAYOUT OF A SYRIAC FRAGMENT: BL ADD. MANUSCRIPT 17.216 - ff. 2-14

RITA SAWAYA
UNIVERSITY OF TORONTO

The manuscript in question is a 7th century historical account nicknamed *Chronicon Maroniticum* or the *Maronite Chronicle* (henceforth: the "Chronicle") that is now in a fragmentary state. This manuscript, consisting of fragments, is a rare 7th century AD Syriac annalistic chronicle that relates events spanning from the time of Alexander the Great (4th century BC) to the first decade of the Umayyad Caliphate (ca 663/4 AD). The text belongs to a genre of Syriac historiography (history writing) known as universal or world history. It typically traces events from the beginning of Creation, of Adam or that of Abraham, to the present time of the author.[1] This suggests that the author of the Chronicle lived in the 7th century, an idea supported by the apparent contemporary date of the extant fragment. From the account in the latter part of the Chronicle, several scholars suggested that the Chronicler was probably a Maronite, and since several events he relates take place in Jerusalem, it could be possible for him to have been stationed in Jerusalem during the second half of the 7th century. The end of the Chronicle is missing. However, assuming that the Chronicler was contemporary or near contemporary of the events and people he tendentiously describes in the Umayyad period[2], and based on the Chalcedonian affinity of the Maronites deduced from the text, the Chronicle would have been completed between 644 and at the latest before or by 680. For the earlier periods, the Chronicle's principal sources are Eusebius of Cæsarea' Chronicle and the Ecclesiastical History of Theodoret[3]. It is noteworthy that the Chronicle is 'the earliest Syriac text to refer to Eusebius' work, and that its author supplemented the Eusebian material with information from other sources and notes on the history of the Maronites. He continued it until his own epoch, adding notes on the history of the Arabs.[4]

THE IMPORTANCE OF THE CHRONICLE

The physical state of the Chronicle is codicologically problematic, as it is fragmented and damaged, which compromises the integrity both, of the codex and of its textual content. The text survives in three manuscript portions presently dispersed across three continents, though believed to originally have belonged to the same codex. The main portion is in Europe. It consists of 13 folios (ff. 2-14) presently housed at the British Library (BL Add MS 17.216)[5]. A first hands-on look at the chronicle revealed that manuscript BL Add. 17.216 is indeed severely mutilated and fragmentary as mentioned by several scholars[6]. Textually, it lacks the section preceding Alexander's death, and probably the section after 663/4 CE abruptly ending with a detailed description of the Muslim invasion of Byzantine Anatolia in 664. A first flyleaf thought to belong to the Chronicle is presently in Asia, housed in the Saint-Petersburg National Library of Russia, under the shelf-mark Cod. Syr. 1, f. 1. Another suggested fragment, DSF5, is in North Africa, housed at Deir al-Suryān in Egypt (See below Frag. DSF5 r and v)[7]. The text section of the Chronicle that is based on Eusebius of Cæsarea's *Ecclesiastical History* is missing before the death of Alexander the Great, with the exception of the St Petersburg flyleaf, Syriac 1, which contains a muddled rendition of the beginning of the Chronicle, including a calendrical computation of the years from Adam to the Anno Græcorum of Seleucus. There is a substantial lacuna of parts relating events from the late fourth century to the mid-seventh inclusive. The fragment is acephalous and anurous, with no extant colophon, and its title, author and place of completion remain unknown. It acquired its nickname based on an anecdote in its latter part that is undoubtedly contemporaneous with the scribe who wrote it. The anecdote to which this fragment owes its now global renown is that of Caliph Mu'āwiya arbitrating in a dogmatic dispute between two groups of clergy from among the greater diverse Syriac community, one Maronite and the other Syriac Orthodox.

Fig. 1: Fig. 1a – (Left) Spine with raised bands; Fig. 1b – (Right) Head of composite manuscript BL Add. 17.216. Photos ©Rita Sawaya, June 2023.[8]

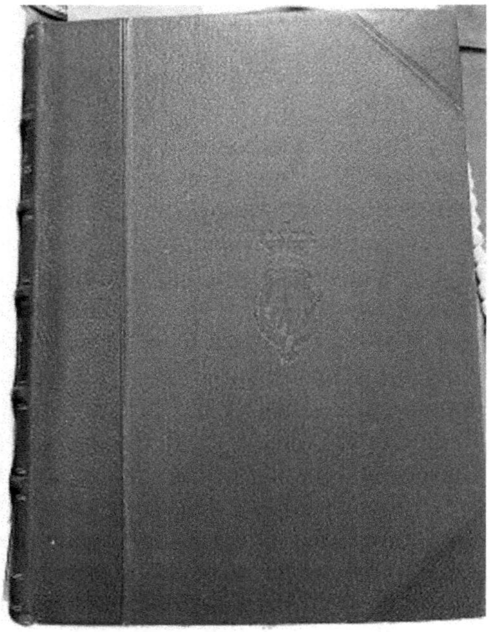

Fig. 2. Back cover – with BM emblem of Composite manuscript BL Add. 17.216.

Fig. 3– Back cover – with BM emblem of Composite manuscript BL Add. 17.216.
British Royal Coat of Arms on Composite Manuscript BL Add. 17.216.[9]

This fragment is famous mostly because it is among the earliest accounts mentioning the transition from the *Khulafā' al-Rāshidīn*'s Caliphate to that of the Umayyads' with their founder Mu'āwiya bin Abi Sufiyān. It relates peculiar anecdotes about him and his reign, and provides important historical data, including and not limited to information on inter-Syriac Christian relations, broader inter-Christian relations, and on Christian-Muslim relations in the formative period of the Umayyad caliphate. The Chronicle is still the earliest source that mentions Mu'āwiya's accession to the throne with several peculiarities related to him and *jihād* as holy Islamic war. It mentions Mu'āwiya's founding of the Umayyad caliphate in Jerusalem, his reception of the pledges of the tribal chieftains, his prayer at Golgotha and by the Virgin Mary's Tomb in Gethsemane, close to the Temple Mount, his refusal to "wear a crown like other kings of the world", and his emission of coinage that does not bear the cross. The final two fragments impart narratives for the years 658-664. This latter part of the Chronicle captivated the attention of eminent Syriac scholars and historians, who paid much attention to its accounts on early Islam.[10]

Fig. 4 – Headband of Composite manuscript BL Add. 17.216.

THE CHRONICLE AS A FRAGMENT

Though badly damaged and fragmented, the Chronicle holds a wealth of information as a material object. To date, scholars' interest gravitated towards its textual content, focusing mostly on its latter section dealing with Byzantine and Islamic events of the 7th century. While the unique narratives provided by the Chronicle's text make it a rare historical document, its materiality as a fragment could add important information to its story. Considering the Chronicle as a fragment and a material object, one thinks of the codex it used to be a part of and of its new physical state as a fragment. "Fragments not only relate to the whole they originally belonged to, but also to a whole that the history of fragmentation created. They can be found in the bindings of printed books, and thus book history must also come to terms with manuscript fragments. By starting with fragments as such, shifting the focus from fragments as fragments of *something* to fragments as *frag-*

ments of, we can investigate a range of historical phenomena beyond simply the entire codex from which (some) fragments were separated. We can explore phenomena of reuse, such as the binding of fragments into host volumes the circumstances of a broken book, or the interest that moved someone to excise an initial."[11] The codicological and palaeographical study of the Chronicle are also fragmentological, focusing on its particular status as fragment and the hidden stories it can potentially tell. As Christoph Flüeler and William Duba maintain, fragmentology is a 'transdisciplinary' field of study in the humanities, though not 'wholly independent,' it has 'a subject matter and a methodology of its own.'[12] As such, fragmentology can benefit the study of Syriac fragments, and in this case, the study of the materiality of the Chronicle. Among the material features explored in studying the physicality of manuscript fragments, are such elements such as the substrate, or writing support, the inks and other markings, stitch points, and page layout.

This paper is part of a larger study of the fragments that constitute the Chronicle. It focuses on page layout technique used in producing it.

The main objective of this preliminary study is twofold: Firstly, to highlight the page layout as one of several important features of a fragment's material individualities, which contributes to contextualising it materially and technically. Secondly, this study attempts, through an examination of the page layout, to clarify the Chronicle's relation to DSF5, one of two fragments (DSF5 and Cod. Syr. 1) that are deemed to belong to it.[13] To this end, we use as reference Françoise Briquel-Chatonnet's study of early Syriac page layout design and specs from the 5th to the 7th centuries.[14] Following a brief descriptive codicological synopsis of the Chronicle, this paper then considers the layout and visual balance that the copyist sought to achieve, with a focus on the different techniques that he would have used to accomplish this task.

In so doing we attempt to deduce the pagination, folio layout and preparation techniques of a damaged Syriac fragment– in this case, those of the Chronicle – based on Françoise Briquel-Chatonnet's standardization of Syriac pagination of the same time-period. In this paper, we will test the abovementioned standards' applicability to Syriac fragments, using this method to clarify the relation of two fragments (in this case DSF5 and ff. 2-14 of manuscript BL Add. 17.216).

CODICOLOGICAL SYNOPSIS

The "Chronicle" presently dwells in a composite rebound codex of miscellaneous fragments at the British Library in London, shelf-marked British Library Add. MS 17.216 (See Figs. 1, 2, 3 and 4). This composite manuscript is a 53-folio codex consisting of a group of various fragments from different manuscripts and codices. Its fragments were rebound at the British Museum in the 1800s' as part of the library's Additional Collection[15]. Within this composite codex, thirteen folios (ff. 2r to 14v) that constitute the Chronicle are a fragment that used to belong to a late antique codex of an annalistic chronicle, a literary genre known as world history, as abovementioned.

A main feature of this fragment is that portions of it are dispersed across two different continents. Tracking the journey of the Chronicle's dismemberment and separation is part of a provenance study that falls outside the scope of this paper.

Originally bound in a codex prior to its fragmentation and rebinding, the Chronicle's substrate is made of parchment with 13 damaged folios that belong to one codicological unit. The damaged folios seem to have been stabilized (see Figs. 5, 6, 8-17) at the British Museum and were set into smooth vellum-like modern parchment frames to form new 'hybrid folios' of 278 x 190 mm, measuring the external dimensions of these modern frames. These frames protect the fragile fragments from further deterioration. They are smoother in texture than the Chronicle's parchment folios and are quite sturdy; their surfaces were incised with precision to fit the fragments' contours to which the latter fragments were meticulously glued (see Figs. 5, 6, 8-17). The type of glue remains to be studied, as are other elements, including and not limited to: The dark brown and yellowish-brown blotches, holes, tears, creases, the inks used by the scribe, and the parchment skin species[16].

THE CRHONICLE AND ITS IMMEDIATE NEIGHBOURS

The Chronicle is the second of 21 fragments (fragments with a number and name are indicated henceforth as Frag.) within manuscript BL Add. 17.216. A more detailed description and elaborate study of the Chronicle and its immediate neighbours is in progress. Meanwhile the list of fragments populating BL Add. MS 17.216 are as follows: Frag. 1: f. 2r-v (1 folio); Frag. 2: "Maronite Chronicle" ff. 2-14 (13 folios); Frag. 3. ff. 15-16 (2 folios); Frag. 4: ff. 18r-23v (5 folios); Frag. 5: ff. 24r-25v (2 folios); Frag. 6: ff. 26r –27v (2 folios); Frag. 7: 28r-30v (3 folios); Frag. 8: 31r (no writing), 31v-33r (Creed of Philoxenus with decorated page head; two hands, the most recent cursive, written maladroitly in the heading space indicating the content) (32v no writing, four hollow brown circles traced a in square array); Frag 9: ff. 34r-41v (unclear writing), note ff. 39 v and 40 r (palimpsest); Frag. 10: ff. 42r-v (1 folio); Frag 11: 43r and v (no writing, only brown stains); Frag. Ff. 12: 44r- 44v (1 folio); Frag 13: ff. 45r-v; Frag. 14: f. 46r-v; (1 folio) Frag. 15: f. 47r-v; (1 folio); Frag. 16:

Fig. 5 – f. 2r – BL Add. MS 17.216.

Fig. 6 – ff. 3v, 4r – BL Add. MS 17.216.

f. 48r-v (1folio) (no writing on v, straight incisions and yellowish-brown stain on the bottom); Frag. 17: f. 49r-v (1 folio) (no writing on v, with yellowish brown stain scattered); Frag. 18: f.50r-v (writing in black ink: two lines upside down); Frag. 19: f. 51r-v (1 folio) (writing on v: Syriac, vertically top to bottom and more recent

"D" and "L" in capital letters at the centre of the fragment; Frag. 20: f. 52r-v (1 folio) (no writing: only stains and wholes); Frag. 21: f. 53r (only one line scribbled and a horizontal decorative wave at the top of the page that stops before missing part both in black ink, i.e., written after missing part was fragmented, and v (unintelligible word 5 word-like scribble in black ink; a large dark brown blotch and yellowish-brown stains, tears, small holes, and two-column pagination frame lines traced in lead).

PAGINATION

Manuscript fragments can present a plethora of challenges, both in their physical analysis and their textual study. The types of challenges that codicologists face in studying fragments depend on several factors pertaining to the degree and type of damage a codex, or a fragment has undergone. Certain fragment deteriorations can impede the examination of codicological features like layout and pagination. For instance, fragments that used to belong to a

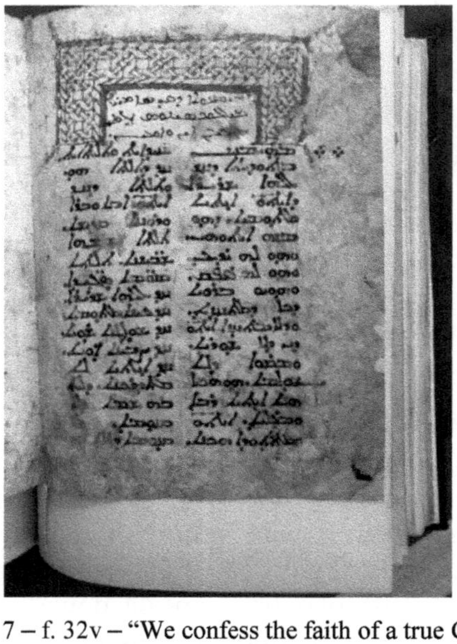

Fig. 7 – f. 32v – "We confess the faith of a true God" Philoxenus of Mabbug (Creed) – BL Add. MS 17.216.

codex could be totally detached from a quire, torn, trimmed or cut for rebinding, and could have parts of the folio surface missing. The Chronicle's folios– as can be seen in the photos (Figs. 5, 6; 8-17)– show torn sections, missing edges and parts, and other deteriorations, which present a challenge when trying to study their page layout. Although it could help to have several folios that are more complete, one could hope to find less damaged ones to work on, as the types and degrees of deterioration can still make it difficult to study the layout. In such a case, a systematic study on Syriac page layout design could be useful in attempting to solve some of the unknowns about the fragment in question.

While turning the folios of manuscript BL Add. 17.216, one notices that they bear modern pagination from 1 to 53 in Indian numerals, written in lead on the recto of each folio on the top outer corner of the header. An initial set of modern folio numbers were rectified and marked with strikethroughs, and new numbers were added (varying by ±1) marked close to the barred one. On some folios (e.g., ff. 10r, 12) there are three numbers: Two page numbers with strikethroughs and an additional rectified one. An additional Indian numeral that is ±1 digit than the rectified number that is at the top external corner and two digits less that the strikethrough number. The bottom numbers were marked by hand in lead at the centre of the footer as is apparent, for example on f. 9r (Fig. 9), where we see the number 8, and on f. 10r (Fig. 10) where the number in the centre of the footer shows a 9. These numbers have no strikethrough marks. For e.g. f 9r (Fig. 9) numbered in the top outer corner as 9 with a 10 strikethrough, and bears an 8 at the centre of its footer.

Some folios were entirely vertically severed, and from the little that remains we can barely see the first letter of the left column. They were cut out very close to the inner margin (see f. 11r: Fig. 15 and f. 13 r and v: Fig. 16-17). It could be that pagination was rectified after the removal some of folios (severed folios). The cut does not show sign of tearing, but rather suggest the use of a sharp-edged instrument like a scalpel. On some folios, we also see other modern pagination written in lead that does not follow the page number sequence, like the number 302 in the footer of f. 7r left of the tear (See Fig. 8: f. 7r (detail)).

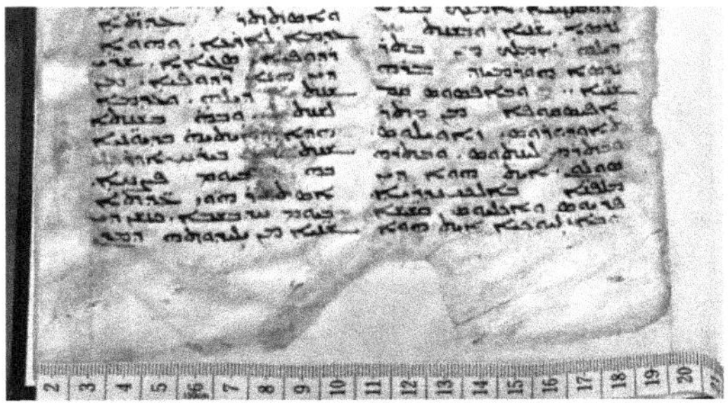

Fig. 8 – f. 7r (detail) – BL Add. MS 17.216.

Also noteworthy is the presence of unnumbered empty smooth modern parchment folios and paper separating several folios in the rebound manuscript.

Fig. 10 – f. 9v-10r – BL Add. MS 17.216

Fig. 9 – f. 9r – BL Add. MS 17.216.

Fig. 11– f. 7r – BL Add. MS 17.216.

PAGE LAYOUT AND DIMENSIONS

The original folio dimensions are not readily visible. Written in black and red ink, in Estrangela script, the text is laid out in a bi-column format, with 32 to 34+ lines per page (Figs 9, 10: f. 9 r, v: 33 lines), 6 mm apart, and 2 to 4 words per line. Regarding the inner margins: Some fragments were rebound in such a manner that the original sewing is mostly hidden in the new spine and the stitching punctures can be examined more clearly, if the present codex were to be unbound, or non-invasively examined using a micro-CT scan[17]. Some of the folios entirely detached, are framed away from the spine within the restorative rectangular modern parchment-frames used in conservation. For example, the inner margin of the first folio (f. 2) of the Chronicle hides in the spine of the rebound manuscript. Similarly to f. 2, folios 8, 9, 10, 14, for example, are completely detached from the original quire, missing their inner margins and inserted within the rebinding vellum-frame. Folios 11, 12 and 13 have been cut out from the Chronicle fragment. Folio 8's inner margin disappears in the rebinding but is detached from folios 9 and 7.

Examples of page surfaces showing dimension inconsistencies: for f. 2= 250x170 mm; f. 7= 250x184 mm; f. 8= 250x150 mm; 245 x 170 mm; f.9= 260x170; f. 10= 240x 170 mm; f. 12= 255x170 mm. The inconsistent page surface measurements noted in these examples from the Chronicle demonstrate the unreliability of these incomplete fragments to obtain sound page dimensions.

This leads us to attempt calculation based on a more reliable element, namely the writing surface, which presents more consistency.[13] The dimensions can in some cases be derived from the size of the double columns on the writing surface. The writing surface is quasi constant, e.g., f. 2 = 198 x 169 mm, the inner column width is 7.1 mm, the outer column width is 6.9mm, the inter-column width 10 mm. For the rest of this page's measurements we must consider the inconsistencies due to the damage. The rest of the margins are respectively 35 mm for the lower margin, 5 to 10 mm for the upper margin, 20 to 50 mm for the outer margin

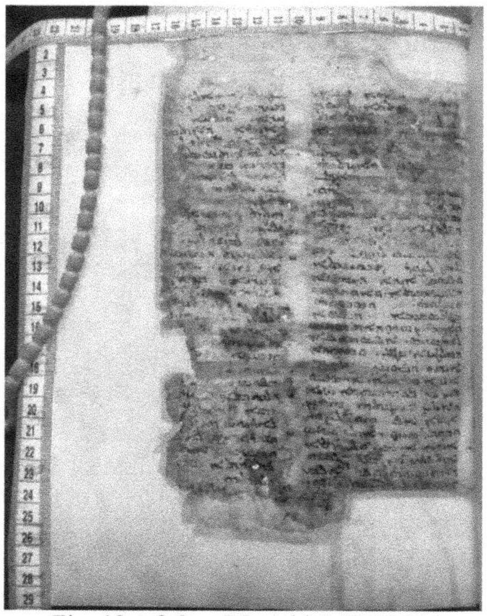

Fig. 12 – f. 8r – BL Add. MS 17.216.

Fig. 13 – f. 8v – BL Add. MS 17.216

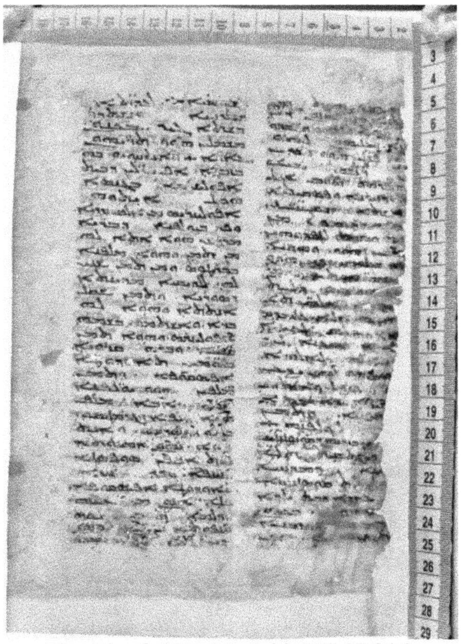

Fig. 14 – f. 10r– BL Add. MS 17.216.

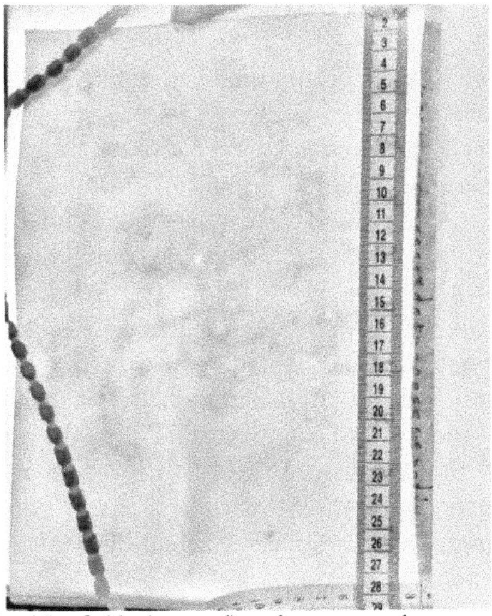

Fig. 15 – f. 11r (severed) and empty modern parchment separator on light sheet – BL Add. MS 17.216.

(it seems deteriorated), and close to 1 mm for the inner margin (which is also deteriorated). The writing area is subdivided into two columns each approximately 72 mm (right) to 75 (left) mm wide with the inter-column margin approximately 12 to 15 mm wide.

Measuring f. 7v, that has somewhat more complete folio edges and writing surface: The page dimensions are 250 x 182 mm; 34 lines with 6 mm interlinear space; the writing surface is 198 x 153 mm, with the inner column width of 75 mm, the outer column width of 68 mm, and the inter-column space measuring 10 mm.

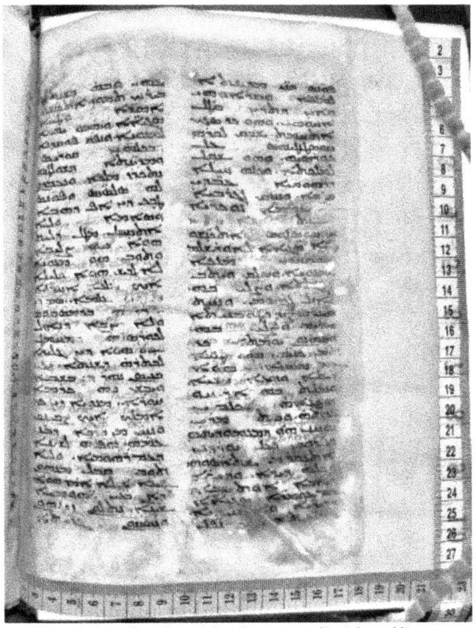

Fig. 16 – f. 12v-13r (severed) (detail) – BL Add. MS 17.216.

Fig. 17 – f. 13 v (severed) and14r – BL Add. MS 17.216.

For fragment DSF5: Per the codicological data in Sebastian Brock's description, the folio dimensions are 200x170+, the layout is a bi-column, conforming with that of the Chronicle, with the inner column measuring 71 mm, the outer column 82 mm, and the inter-column margin width measuring 10 mm. The writing area's height is unknown, with its width measuring 154mm. The columns count 22+ lines per page and interlinear space is 6 mm. In his description of DSF5, Brock suggests "it seems likely that this is part of the 'Maronite Chronicle', very poorly preserved in Br. Libr. Add. 17,216, ff.2-14," based on similarities in script and dimensions, which he deems "would seem to fit well.[18]

From the writing surface measurement samples of the more or less constant

Frag. DSF5 r - Deir al-Suryan Fragment 5 recto – ©Sebastian Brock and Lucas Van Rompay, p. 611.

Frag. DSF5 v - Deir al-Suryan Fragment 5 recto – ©Sebastian Brock and Lucas Van Rompay, p. 612.

elements, i.e. mainly the column widths of the writing space, we see similarities between the Chronicle and fragment DSF5. The writing surface width of folio 7v is close to 153 mm, that of the DSF5 is 150mm, with a difference of 3 mm. The similarity between the two fragments in question is namely in the column widths. The inner column width of DSF5 measures 71 mm, the inter-column space 10mm and the outer column 69mm. Whereas for f. 7v: the inner column width is 75, the inter-column space 10 mm and the outer column width 68mm. These measurements are fairly close. For more accuracy, it would take numerous measurements to detect a pattern and an acceptable margin of error in order to confirm the relation between the two fragments. Other data could be useful to do so. Combined with the textual that was edited and translated by Sebastian Brock, DSF5 could complement the textual lacunas in the Chronicle. The codicological data based on pagination, combined with other codicological and paleographic data, could contribute to corroborate that DSF5 belongs to the Chronicle.[19]

According to Briquel-Chatonnet's Syriac pagination and page layout standards, "in the same manuscript, the height/width ratio is approximately the same for the size of the page and for that of the writing surface and the slight irregularities can be explained by a certain variation in the height of the writing surface. From one manuscript to another, this ratio remains within a range of 1.2 to 1.7."[20] Which makes the general appearance for the page almost invariable. The reason for the use of the bi- or even tricolumn layout, as we see in the example studied by Briquel-Chatonnet, is that of "reinforcing the impression of verticality" as is evinced in the page layout of BL Add. MS 14.452 (509 Ad).[21]

The Chronicle falls within the medium size codex category, which justifies the bicolumn. One notices that the larger the size of the Syriac manuscript, the more the column numbers, with a maximum of three; and the smaller the manuscript the less columns in the writing surface with a minimum of one, as Briquel-Chatonnet demonstrates (in BL Add. 17126 (510-511 AD) and BL Add. 12150. The threshold from which a writing surface passes to two columns is 100 to 110 mm width, and the 110 mm allows for two columns each between 50 to 55 mm, wide (or at a minimum 40 mm as for BL Add. 17176) with the inter-column space ranging between 10 and 18 mm. In the case of the Chronicle, the width is 170 mm, and the width of column is 70-75 mm with that of the inter-column space being 12-15 mm.[22]

Following the page layout proportion metrics in Briquel-Chatonnet's study, since the margins are also arranged consistently, from largest to smallest, one can find the bottom margin, the outer margin, the top margin and the inner margin, which corresponds more or less to what we find in a modern book. However, if this order is constant, the two middle margins, outside and at the top of the page, can sometimes have the same width, which applies to the Chronicle (Fig. 10: f. 10r). Conversely, the bottom margin is often double or even triple the width of the inner margin, the narrowest. This proportion could hypothetically apply to the relation between the inner and bottom margin in the Chronicle, despite the lacking data for the inner margin widths in the fragments, due to rebinding on the one side and due to the unevenness of inner margins in the detached folios.

LAYOUT TECHNIQUE

Rather than using the common method of applying pigments in the corners of each column, the Chronicle's copyist seems to have used pencil ruling to delimit vertical margins, as well as the first and the last, as we see, for example, in Fig. 8: f. 7v. The absence of lines within the column writing space applies to the Chronicle, as is common in very early Syriac manuscripts. The same seems to apply for DSF5, from the photos of the fragment in Brock and van Rompay's catalogue.[23]

It is not possible to verify in this case whether the ruler lines correspond exactly to the stitching. However, in spite of the fragmentation, the overall visual balance of the pagination in the Chronicle suggests regularity in line justification by the copyist. As indicated above, there are 2 to 4 words per line in each column. Briquel-Chatonnet explains that this line justification in early Syriac manuscripts was obtained, by adjusting the width of the inter-word space on each line. The words can be very far apart or with very little to no space, with some words stretched to fill the gaps, and filler signs used as segment- or paragraph-ending markers were also used at the end of a line to obtain visual balance (Fig. 16: f12v).

The Chronicle's copyist respected the vertical limits of the written surface, maintained column and inter-column margin regularity. Sometimes, in the Chronicle, the copyist deliberately extended certain letters beyond the right border of either column, as is shown for the letters ܠ ,ܟ ,ܬ , ܒ, ܐ, accentuating his calligraphic style (See Fig. 8: f. 7 (detail), and DSF5 r and v above). As Sebastian Brock pointed out regarding the similarity of the script with the Chronicle, this is obvious from the photos of Frag. DSF5.[24] This overflow by a few millimetres is paleographically characteristic of the scribe's calligraphic style and its recurrence embellishes the text rendering as is evident from the photos. As noted by Briquel-Chatonnet, while 'the width of the written surface is regular in a manuscript, the height varies,'[25] and so can the number of lines that could increase at the bottom (see for exampleFig. 9: f. 9v). In effect, one can deduce from the existing folios, that the copyist of the Chronicle respected the mark, which indicates the start of the column, with some protrusion at the bottom of the columns beyond its lower limits and into the footer margin, by two or three lines.

A common aspect noticed by Briquel-Chatonnet is the significant variation of the number of lines per column within the same manuscript (in BL Add. MS 17182 it varies from 32 to 41, an excessive eight lines) and in the Chronicle it starts at 32 and can reach 34 lines per column, with only a variation of 2 lines, which makes the height of the lower margin also quite variable, despite it always remaining much higher than the others. This explains the extra height of the footer margin in the page layout. The column overflow variation in the Chronicle is not excessive, as the copyist adjusted the space between the writing lines, thus maintaining a rather constant and visually balanced written surface. Although the Chronicle does not seem to have been a luxury manuscript, and despite it being fragmentary and damaged, it maintains a visual balance that is aesthetically appealing to the eyes.

This demonstrates the copyist's expertise in page layout planning and design, and his resolute-ness in respecting this Syriac page layout model. Another notable feature is the tendency of the lines to move up from right to left, and this is increases as the writing fills the page from top to bottom, which is not a pronounced feature in the Chronicle.

The page layout of the Chronicle conforms to that of the medium-sized bicolumn of the classical layout pattern in early Syriac manuscripts. The beauty of the bicolumn layout that we see in the Chronicle and the harmonious visual layout of early Syriac texts were characteristic of Syriac manuscripts up until the 19th century. Françoise Briquel-Chatonnet's systematic detailed study of early Syriac page layouts and techniques, and her survey of standard Syriac page design features serve an essential reference when performing comparative analyses of Syriac page layouts, as was demonstrated in this study, through the applicability to the Chronicle fragment and to Frag. DSF5. It was useful in our attempt to study the relation between these two fragments. Such reliable standardizations provides reliable models that can be useful for the codicological analysis of Syriac manuscripts in general and Syriac fragments in particular.

NOTES

1 Amir Harrak, GEDSH 2011, 2018; Muriel ebié and Antoine Borrut 2009; David Dumville 2002; Sebastian Brock 1979; Karl Heinrich Krueger 1976.

2 Andrew Palmer 1993 ;J. B. Chabot 1955; Theodor Nöldeke 1875.

3 James Howard-Johnston, *Witnesses to a World Crisis: Historians and Histories of the Middle East in the Seventh Century*, (Oxford: Oxford University Press, 2010), p. 175.

4 Witold Witakowski , "Historiography, Syriac," in *Historiography, Syriac*, edited by Sebastian P. Brock, Aaron M. Butts, George A. Kiraz and Lucas Van Rompay, https://gedsh.bethmardutho.org/Historiography-Syriac.

5 Many thanks to Michael Erdmann, Head of the Middle Eastern and Central Asian Collections, to Eugenio Falcioni, Lucia Noor Melita and the MECARR team for facilitating research of Syriac manuscripts at the British Library.

6 For instance, M. Breydy (1990) 'Das Chronikon des Maroniten Theophilus ibn Tuma'. Journal of Oriental and African Studies 2: 34-43; S. Brock (1984) 'Syriac sources for the seventh-century history'. In: Syriac perspectives on Late Antiquity, ed. S.P. Brock (Collected Studies Series, 199). London: VII = Brock, S.P. (1976) 'Syriac sources for the seventh-century history'. Byzantine and modern Greek studies 2: 17-36; M. Debié (2015) L'écriture de l'histoire en syriaque: Transmissions interculturelles et constructions identitaires entre hellénisme et Islam (Late antique history and religion, 12). Leuven - Paris - Bristol: 546-548; R. Hoyland (1997) Seeing Islam as others saw it: A survey and evaluation of Christian, Jewish and Zoroastrian writings on early Islam (Studies in Late Antiquity and early Islam, 13). Princeton: 135-139; H. Lammens (1899) 'Qays al-Mārūnī aw aqdam ta'rīkh li-l-kitbat al-Mawārina'. Al-Machriq 2: 265-268; A. Palmer (1993) The seventh century in the West-Syrian chronicles, including two seventh-century Syriac apocalyptic texts (Translated texts for historians, 15). Liverpool: 29-35; Jan van Ginkel, *Encyclopedia of the Medieval Chronicle*, 2016; Leiden, Koninklijke, Brill, NV, 2010; Howard Johnston, 10. Debié, Muriel. "Writing History as 'Histoires': The Biographical Dimension of East Syriac Historiography." *Writing "True Stories,"* 9:43–75. Turnhout: Brepols Publishers, 2010, p. 675; David Dumville 2002; Sebastian Brock 1979; Karl Heinrich Krueger 1976.

7 Brock 1979; Brock-Van Rompay 2014, pp. 3-4. Frag. DSF5 r (top) &v (bottom) - Deir al-Suryan Fragment 5 recto – ©Sebastian Brock and Lucas Van Rompay, *Catalogue of the Syriac Manuscripts and Fragments in the Library of Deir Al-Surian, Wadi Al-Natrun (Egypt)*. Leuven: Uitgeverij Peeters en Departement Oosterse Studies, 2014, pp. 611-612.

8 Unless otherwise indicated, all photo credits of the Chronicle and BL Add. MS are © Rita Sawaya, BL, London, June 2023, with permission to publish from British Library.

9 This is the British Museum version of the British Royal coat of arms of the Kingdom of England is placed at the centre of the back read leather cover. Usually, the Royal Coat of Arms of the United Kingdom depicts a central shield with the three lions, the Scottish lion, and the Irish harp, supported by a lion and a unicorn. On the cover of BL Add. MS 17.216, the Royal Coat of arms was stamped on the red leather back cover. It is headed with the Royal crest without the habitual crowned lion standing on top of it with its body in profile facing left and its face in frontal position. The Royal Crest usually rests on a Royal helm, not represented here. Also absent is the manting that flanks the help and crown, and the dexter and sinister supporters, a crowned lion and a unicorn standing on their hind legs with their front legs on the shield, as well as the bottom compartment with the Motto in French in block letters "DIEU ET MON DROIT." The Most Noble Order of the Garter, a belt symbolizing the order of chivalry founded by Edward III in 1348, circumscribes the central shield. It is usually circular, with a small space separating it from the shield, is, but on BL Add. MS 17.216 it is vertical ovoid, with the motto: "HONI SOIT QUI MAL Y PENSE" in Anglo-Norman for "Shame on him who thinks evil of it." The quartered shield shows a variant in the contours that shape it. Its quarters The first and fourth emblems, diagonally opposite, designate England with the three seated

usually golden) lions on top of each other, a heraldic device; the second shows the unicorn, Scotland's national animal and symbol of purity and strength; and the third, Ireland with the Irish harp, symbol of Irish music and culture.

[10] E. W. Brooks, "*Chronicon maroniticum*", *Chronica minora pars secunda, textus*, CSCO 3, 1904, 43-74. J.-B. Chabot (1904) (tr.) Chronica minora. Volume Two (Corpus scriptorum Christianorum Orientalium, 4: Scriptores Syri, 4). Paris - Leipzig: 35-57.

[11] "Fragments and Fragmentology," Ed: Christoph Flüeler (Fribourg), William Duba (Fribourg), in *Fragmentology: A Journal for the Study of Medieval Manuscript Fragments*, Fribourg, Switzerland, Vol. 1, 2018, pp. 2-3. Fragmentsand_Fragmentology_editorial.pdf.

[12] The neologism "fragmentology" was coined by Christoph Flüeler in 2014 in Fribourg as part of the *Fragmentarium* project, and shortly after David Rundle from the University of Essex announced the "the Age of Fragmentology" as a novelty subfield in manuscript stuc'ies. Id. Ibid. p. 3.

[13] The relation with Cod. Syr. 1 will dealt with in the larger study.

[14] "La mise en page dans les manuscrits syriaques d'après les anciens manuscrits." *Manuscripta Orientalia* 9 (2003), pp. 3–13.

[15] Wright, William. *Catalogue of the Syriac Manuscripts in the Library of the U. of Cambridge*. 1872, p. 1041. Piscataway, NJ: Gorgias Press, 2002.

[16] See e.g. Vnouček, Jiri (2019) *The Language of Parchment: Tracing the evidence of changes in the methods of manufacturing parchment for manuscripts with the help of visual analyses.* PhD thesis, University of York. Also, see Vnouček, Jiří. 2021. "Not All That Shines like Vellum Is Necessarily So." *Care and Conservation of Manuscripts* 17: 27–60. Fiddyment, Sarah, Matthew D. Teasdale, Jiří Vnouček, Élodie Lévêque, Annelise Binois, and Matthew J. Collins. 2019. "So You Want to Do Biocodicology? A Field Guide to the Biological Analysis of Parchment." *Heritage Science* 7 (1): 35. Reed, Ronald. *Ancient Skins, Parchments and Leathers*, London-New York: Seminar Press, 1972.

[17] Documentary featuring researchers Alexandra Gillespie, Jessica Lockhart et al., in a multi-organizational collaborative initiative for tomography CT-scanning of codices and books, performed by researchers from the "Hidden Stories: Books Along the Silk Roads" Project from the Old Books New Science Lab at the University of Toronto at Mississauga. The video is titled "Inside the scans: Exploring four books using computed tomography (CT) Inside the scans: Exploring four books using computedtomography(CT). https://youtu.be/Gsm7L6tuSZs?si=MQPXS4SrVXhigPrO.

[18] Sebastian Brock, Lucas van Rompay. Catalogue of the Syriac Manuscripts and Fragments in the Library of Deir Al-Surian, Wadi Al-Natrun (Egypt). Leuven: Uitgeverij Peeters en Departement Oosterse Studies, 2014, pp. 373-375, and photos of DSF5 r and v respectively, pp. 711-712;

[19] An in-depth paleographical analysis of the scripts falls beyond the confines of this paper, as do ink and biocodicological substrate analyses, all of which could contribute to comparing that DSF5 with the Chronicle fragment.

[20] My translation of See Françoise Briquel Chatonnet. "La mise en page dans les manuscrits syriaques d'après les anciens manuscrits." *Manuscripta Orientalia* 9 (2003), p. 3.

[21] *Id. Ibid.* p. 10.

[22] *Loc. cit.*

[23] Sebastian Brock and Lucas van Rompay, op. cit., pp. 373-375, photos of DSF5, pp. 611 Fragt. 5r, 612 Fragt. 5v.

[24] *Loc. cit.*

THE MONGOL INVASIONS OF NORTH MESOPOTAMIA— A TRANSLATION AND ANALYSIS OF GEWARGIS WARDA'S *ON KARAMLISH*

JAMES TOMA
UNIVERSITY OF TORONTO

The Mongol incursions into Northern Mesopotamia during the mid-1230s have been somewhat overshadowed in contemporary studies, due in part to the dearth of sources from that period and a predominant focus on subsequent sieges post-1258. Recently, scholars have begun to analyze primary sources to discern nuances that may shed light on dating and other elements, aiming to elucidate the pre-1258 period. This has illuminated a significant gap in our understanding of events, particularly in lesser-studied regions like the Nineveh Plain. This article aims to present an edition and English translation of Gewargis Warda's poem "On Karamlish," penned in 1237/8, and to delve into a commentary that elucidates its historical implications concerning the early Mongol invasions in Northern Mesopotamia.

The article reveals that the Mongol invasion resulted in a widespread massacre of the Christian population in the Nineveh Plains, specifically in three Chaldean towns in the Nineveh Plains: Karamlish, Bet Qoqa, and Tesqopa. Gewargis Warda's poem about the invasions provides a valuable perspective that may alleviate the prevailing obscurity related to this period and region.

HISTORICAL OVERVIEW

In 1206, Temujin, a charismatic Mongol tribal leader, was acknowledged as the supreme leader of the Steppe during a *quriltai*[1], receiving the title Genghis Khan, meaning 'fierce ruler'. From 1211 to 1215, he initiated a sequence of military campaigns against three Chinese empires to the east of Mongolia: His-Hsia, Ch'in, and the Sung.[2] By 1218, after annexing China, the Mongols sent their forces westwards, conquering Kara-Khitay and establishing a strategic entry point into Persia (Khwarazm) and the Near East.[3]

According to some narratives, 'Ala-al-Din Muhammad II (d. 1220), the Shah of Khwarazm, executed Genghis Khan's commercial envoys in 1218.[4] In retaliation, the Mongols invaded Khwarazm, capturing major cities including its capital, Utrar, and others like Bukhara, Merv, and Nishapur. However, it is also conceivable that the Shah's action, ordering the killing of the envoys, provided Genghis Khan a pretext for his invasion into Persia and the Near East.[5]

Gaining control over Persia enabled the Mongols to delve deeper into the civilizations of the Near East. Before he died in 1227, Genghis Khan's conquests extended to Georgia, Armenia, Russia, Poland, and Korea, while also solidifying power in China. In a parallel vein, 'Ala-al-Din Muhammad's heir, Jalal al-Din (d. 1231), managed to mend the fragmented empire and recapture territories in western Persia, controlling regions like Kerman, Fars, Iraq, 'Ajami, and Azerbaijan between 1221 and 1230.[6]

Genghis Khan was succeeded by his son Ogedei in 1227. Generally, scholars find that Ogedei's reign marks a period of expansion and relative stability for the Mongols. Karakorum in central Mongolia was his capital. He ventured into Persia to reclaim territories earlier captured by his father. In 1230, sultanate princes from Konya and Kaykobad allied with the Mongols against Jalal-al-Din, decisively defeating the latter's army near Erzincan and considerably weakening his power. Simultaneously, 30,000 Mongol soldiers under Ogedei Khan, commanded by Chormaghan, were dispatched to Persia in the 1230s.[7] Jalal-al-Din, evading the Mongol forces, initially found sanctuary in Tabriz and later in Kura, but he met his end in 1235, while fleeing to Diyarbakir.[8] Following this, the Mongols advanced into Northern Mesopotamia (and maintained their posts in Persia[9]), as will be explored shortly.

Following Jalal-al-Din's demise in 1231, Chormaghan's forces pressed into Northern Mesopotamia, Persia, and the Armenian highlands, seizing and pillaging numerous major cities, such as Bitlis, Ercis, Maragheh, Diyarbakir, Erbil, and the Nineveh Plains. A substantial Christian population from various denominations, including East Syrians, West Syrians, and Armenians, among others, inhabited these areas. Scant primary sources shed light on the Mongolian military campaigns and their impacts on populations throughout the Near East. Of these, one particular source, "On Karamlish" by Gewargis Warda, which offers a perspective from Northern Mesopotamia, is the focus of the following section.

MANUSCRIPTS AND EDITIONS

"On Karamlish," authored by Gewargis Warda, is found in several manuscripts, often located within compilations titled *The Book of the Rose/Warda*—Warda means Rose in Syriac).[10] Aladár Deutsch first published "On Karamlish" in 1895 in his dissertation *Edition Dreier Syrischen Lieder nach einer Handschrift der Berliner Königlichen Bibliothek*, providing a German translation of the poem, along with two others from *The Book of the Rose*, including "On the Rogation of the Ninevites."[11] Subsequently, Heinrich Hilgenfeld published an edition with a German translation of the same poem in 1904, and he also presented eight other poems from *The Book of the Rose*, including poems on famines and religious conversions, "On Mar John the Baptist," "On Mar Tahmazgerd," and "On Mar James the Intercisus."[12] More recently, Pier Borbone has published an edition of "On Karamlish," providing an Italian translation.[13]

The edition and English translation of Gewargis Warda's "On Karamlish" presented herein relies on three manuscripts. Most of the manuscripts derives from the Telkeppe collection. The initial manuscript is currently under the shelf mark name Qalb-al-Aqdas Chaldean Church (QACCT), 00032, Folios 222v-224v, dated to October 2, 1488.[14] To the best of my knowledge, this manuscript—despite lacking a portion of the latter verses (vv. 64-74)—is the oldest extant poem of Warda and serves as the basis for vv. 1-63. The subsequent verses, 63-71, are included thereafter, and based on QACCT 00035,

Folio 358r, and the final verses (71-74) are based on QACCT 00036, Folios 63v-64r. Alongside these primary texts, additional manuscripts have been scrutinized for corroboration or parallel assessment, including Berlin. 65 (Ms. Orient. Fol. 619). However, QACCT 00032 is predominantly more informative on the subject.

The edition and English translation of Warda's poem is made of 74 verses.[15] Although the original document and its oldest witness (QACCT 00032) do not incorporate verse numbers, they have been introduced to facilitate clear referencing and citation, as well as to enhance the structural coherence of the primary text, without compromising the original work's integrity.

GEWARGIS WARDA

Warda's life period is enigmatic and remains a subject of academic discourse. This ambiguity partly stems from observed inconsistencies found in some poems within *The Book of the Rose* attributed to Gewargis Warda. However, it should be noted that only a subset of these poems—chiefly those which discuss later events—has led some scholars to label them as Pseudo-Warda. Nonetheless, this creates a dilemma about the authentication of his later works, given the extensive period of literary output under his name.[16] The historic milieu permeated by famines and diseases—themes also reflected in Warda's poetry—does not naturally support a narrative of such an elongated lifespan and consistent productivity. The duration of time between Warda's composition of "On Karamlish" (1236/7) and "*Onītha* of the Catholicoi Fathers of the East,"[17] ܥܘܢܝܬܐ ܕܐܒܗܬܐ ܩܬܘܠܝܩܐ ܕܡܕܢܚܐ, which covers up to the reign of Patriarch Timothy II (1318-1332) is roughly 81 years. Could it be the compositions of either his contemporaries or disciples, such as Khamis bar Qardaḥe or Gabriel Qamsa, which integrated into *The Book of the Rose*? At this point in time, we can only speculate with the limited data available on Gewargis Warda's life and career. Although manuscripts hint at Erbil being Warda's place of birth and an East Syriac priest, the latter end of his life is not entirely clear. Additionally, Abdisho' bar Brikha (d. 1318), the East Syrian legal scholar and compiler omits any mention of Gewargis Warda in his authored bibliography.

STRUCTURE OF THE POEM

"On Karamlish" is written in classical Syriac, with 74 verses in total, the prologue (v. 1) and epilogue (vv. 73-74) do not follow the rhymed syllable structure; instead serving as introduction and conclusion in *onīyāthē*. In the main verses (vv. 2-72), there consists four rhymed seven-syllable lines, a poetic feature characteristic of the *onītha*.[18] "On Karamlish" is made of the following parts:

(1) Introductory Portion (Prologue) (v. 1)
(2) Exposition (vv. 2-7)
(3) Theme 1 (Bet Qoqa) (vv. 8-14)
(4) Theme 2 (Karamlish) (vv.15-51)
(5) Theme 3 (Tesqopa) (52-62)
(6) Theme 4 (Theological motives) (63-72)
(7) Conclusion (Epilogue) (vv. 73-74)

INTRODUCTORY PORTION (V.1)

"On Karamlish" organizes its subject matter systematically. The introductory verse reveals crucial details including the year in which the Mongols arrived in the region, 1547 Greek King (=1236/7) and foreshadows commotion. In the broader literary landscape, this opening is a basic introduction to the subject matter and foreshadows the subsequent theme.

EXPOSITION (VV. 2-7)

The *onītha* draws attention to the events of November 1236/7 and 1237/8, but before doing so, Gewargis Warda informs us that the poem was written one year after the event. It states that, "In the year before this" ܒܫܢܬܐ ܗ̇ܝ ܕܩܕܡ ܗܕܐ there were famines, which indicates that Gewargis Warda wrote the poem in 1237/8. Moreover, the author proceeds into describing that in November, "the first indignation began, and on the fourth day, a rough commotion arose in Erbil" ܬܫܪܝ، ܗܘ ܠܐ ܡܕܝܢܐ ܘܡܫܘܚܬܐ ܕܒܗ ܪܒܝܥܝܐ ܒܐܪܒܝܠ ܗܘܐ ܘܗܠܐ ܩܫܝܐ (v. 3). Our author discloses an account of the devastation wrought in Erbil on November 4. Gewargis Warda shows that Erbil resisted the Mongols, and at some point, they turned to the Nineveh Plains. Gewargis Warda states the following: "There, they killed princes—princes, sons of princes. The nobles fell outside, and horsemen [fell] inside the pits" ܬܡܢ ܩܛܠܘ ܠܐܡܝܪ̈ܐ ܐܡܝܪ̈ܐ ܒܢܝ ܐܡܝܪ̈ܐ ܦܪܝܫܐ ܢܦܠܘ ܒܒܪ ܒܪ̈ܐ ܐܦ ܪ̈ ܠܓܘ ܒܓܘ ܫܘ̈ܦܐ (v. 6). The poem then describes that they then turned to, "the fields like tigers and lionesses ܒܫܩܝܬܐ ܐܝܟ ܢܡܪ̈ܐ ܘܐܪܝܘܬܐ (v. 7), which is a reference to the countryside (i.e., Nineveh Plains), a region our author addresses hereafter.

BET QOQA (vv. 8-14)

Following an introduction to the Mongol invasion and an exposition of their entry into Erbil, this section discusses the tragedies experienced in Bet Qoqa, a Chaldean town in the Nineveh Plains.[19] It states that, "On the morning of the second day, they surrounded Beth Qoqa as clouds full of gloomy darkness and fire-damaging hail" ܒܨܦܪܗ ܕܝܘܡܐ ܬܪܝܢܐ ܚܕܪܘ ܠܒܝܬ ܩܘܩܐ ܐܝܟ ܥܢܢܐ ܕܡܠܝܢ ܚܫܘܟܐ ܘܥܪܦܠܐ ܘܢܘܪܐ ܘܒܪܕܐ ܡܚܒܠܢܐ (v. 8). Here, we are informed that on the second day of the invasion—that is, November 9—Bet Qoqa was invaded. The Mongol advance into Bet Qoqa seems brief, indicating that they stayed in the town for one day.

There is a strong possibility that the Mongols entered Bet Qoqa with the intention to plunder it. For instance, Warda states that the Mongols desecrated the "Holy Temple (=Church)" ܠܗܝܟܠܐ ܩܕܝܫܐ and plundered the relics and graves of the saints (vv. 12-13). These areas described typically house relics crafted from gold and precious minerals. In addition, graves also contained valuable items that the Mongols sought and took. The attention given to Bet Qoqa is brief, potentially due to the rapid nature of the pillage. Warda provides more details over the Nineveh Plains.

KARAMLISH (VV. 15-51)

The fourth and notably most detailed section, to which the poem's concentrate is Karamlish, a Chaldean town in the Nineveh Plains.[20] On Tuesday evening, "they passed through the Great Zab, and in Karamlish, filled with love, they caused a great terror" ܥܒܪܘ ܠܗܘܢ ܠܙܒܐ ܪܒܐ ܘܒܟܪܡܠܝܫ ܡܠܝܬ ܚܘܒܐ ܥܒܕܘ ܗܘܘ ܒܗ̇ ܠܒܘܫܝܐ ܪܒܐ (v. 15). From this, we learn that the Mongols invaded Karamlish on Tuesday, November 10, 1236/7. The author sheds light on horrors that befell Karamlish, offering clues that the poem's audience may be the people of that town.

Furthermore, unlike Bet Qoqa, in Karamlish, not only were churches subjected to pillaging, but houses were also targeted. Warda notes that in the evening the Mongols began in pillaging the houses of the Karamlishites (v. 17). It is evident that the aim was not only to appropriate the people's valuables, but also, by the ensuing evening of November 11, residents suffered separation (vv. 18-19). The Mongols lingered in Karamlish from November 10 to November 15, in contrast to a single day (November 9) in Bet Qoqa.

Why did the Mongols decide to invest their military efforts in Karamlish, as opposed to Erbil or Bet Qoqa? A plausible answer might be that Karamlish functioned as an intersection between Mosul and Erbil, which established as a strategic hub for the invaders. The Mongols likely perceived Karamlish as a centre for extensive plundering, but also for their armies to station in preparation for upcoming incursions across Mesopotamia and Persia.

TESQOPA (vv. 52-62)

The examination progresses, bringing us to the fifth section of the *onītha*. Warda addresses another town the Mongols invaded, Tesqopa, which he acknowledges as having been decimated. The section initiates with the following: "I will mourn over Tesqopa a great and powerful village! Like a bird with a clipped wing, one church was eradicated by the sword" ܒܟܐ ܐܒܟܐ ܠܬܣܩܘܦܐ ܘܣܩܘܦܐ ܩܪܝܬܐ ܪܒܬܐ ܕܬܩܝܦܬܐ ܕܐܝܟ ܨܦܪܐ ܨܦ ܨܦ ܬ ܠܚܪܒܐ ܚܕܐ ܥܕܬܐ ܗܘܬ ܒܣܝܦܐ (v. 54). In the following verse, Warda states the destruction of Tesqopa's church noting the following: "The Church of Mār James the Intercisus: How grievously it suffered! It lamented in agony, and no saviour came to it" ܥܕܬܐ ܕܡܪܝ، ܝܥܩܘܒ ܡܦܣܩܐ ܐܝܟ ܚܫ ܠܗ̇ ܦܩܘܥܐ ܗܘܬ ܒܚܫܐ ܘܡܬܬܢܚܐ ܘܠܐ ܐܬܐ ܠܗ̇ ܦܪܘܩܐ (v. 55). Moreover, while Warda laments the deceased and the destruction of the church, he also provides us with details on how long the Mongols were stationed in Tesqopa. In verse 60, Warda states that the people of Tesqopa were unable to celebrate Christmas and the Epiphany, and they did not fast the fifty-days. Warda continues that the people of Tesqopa also could not celebrate on the day of Hosanna and neither on Easter (v. 61). From these details, we are able to infer that the Mongols were stationed in Tesqopa, according to our author, for several months, chiefly between mid-November and March/April. In liturgical terms, the people of Tesqopa were unable to participate in the feast days from Christmas up to Easter.

THEOLOGICAL MOTIVES (vv. 63-72)

At this juncture, Warda navigates into the theological realm of the *onītha*, embarking with a poignant appeal to God:

> Oh Lord of lords, where is the parable, which is in your vivifying Gospel, about your chosen wheat? You, O Lord, commanded the winds to spare the wheat—royal offspring— for the sake of the wheat, the children of the faithful. Behold! The weeds have grown powerful, and the roots of the wheat have been uprooted! O, judge over all judges, from those whom these are judging. If the churches are uprooted and the monasteries and convents demolished, what then is the edict of this blasphemy, and what is the response of baptism? The hidden mind awoke me and said: "Silence, O wretched one! Your question is loathsome, even more so than your hateful essence!" (vv. 63-67).

Warda embodies a commoner here, engaging in an internal struggle, questioning his faith and his God until his conscience warns him of his misdirection. Consequently, it is implied that the Mongol onslaught on Bet Qoqa, Karamlish and Tesqopa, was so brutal and horrific that others too were led astray by their thoughts amid the devastation, much like Warda until he found restraint.

To further strengthen his previous statements, Warda adds another layer of hope in the poem by further evoking Scripture. Warda states the following:

> "Have you not heard what your Lord said to all the faithful: 'They will hate you and kill you, and offer make you as sacrifices. I shall send you like lambs among the wolves so that they will strangle you! When they kill you in the earth, you will rejoice in my Kingdom with me! The servant is not above his lord, nor is the messenger greater than the one who sent him. Your Lord was killed, and His tomb sealed, yet your mouth persists in its idle chatter! (vv. 68-70).

Warda begins to directly admonish those whose 'your mouth persists in its idle chatter!' who are essentially the East Syrians who have beseeched God, questioning why they have been subjected to such a malevolent, ruinous, and spiteful invasion.

In conclusion, Warda invites the congregation to pursue repentance, resilience, and steadfastness, stating as follows: "You have sinned and transgressed as a wrongdoer. As a transgressor, I speak! I speak spiritually! Have mercy on me and the author! " ܣܟܠܬ ܘܐܣܟܠܬ ܐܝܟ ܡܣܟܠܢܐ ܘܐܡܝܢ ܡܡܠܠ ܐܢܐ ܐܘ ܪܘܚܢܐ ܪܚܡ ܡܣܟܠܢܐ ܡܡܠܠ ܐܢܐ ܥܠܝ ܘܥܠ ܡܪܟܒܢܐ (v. 73).

CONCLUSION

The epilogue seals the *onītha* with a heartfelt dedication and an offering of condolence to the defeated. It culminates in a prayer and plea to God to establish justice for those swallowed by the tide of calamity. It states as follows:

> Have mercy on the oppressed and over the ones who became little in number. Be a guardian and comforter! And praise to you in every tongue and on us your mercies at all times (v. 74).

> ܚܘܣ ܠܛܠܝܡ̈ܐ ܐܘܚܕ ܠܛܠܝܡ̈ܐ ܘܠܒܨܝܪ̈ܐ
> ܗܘܝ ܒܡܢܝܢܐ ܗܘܝ ܡܢܛܪܢܐ ܘܡܒܝܐܢܐ
> ܘܠܟ ܬܫܒܘܚܬܐ ܒܟܠ ܠܫܢܐ ܘܥܠܝܢ
> ܪ̈ܚܡܝܟ ܒܟܠ ܥܕܢ.

FINAL REMARKS

The Mongol incursions into Northern Mesopotamia during the mid-1230s have received relatively limited attention in contemporary scholarship. Extant sources from this period are scarce. However, the few available ones require thorough scholarly examination, in hopes of reconstructing the campaigns and determining the dates of the incursions of Northern Mesopotamia.[21] This article has provided an overview of these Mongol incursions of Northern Mesopotamia, followed by a presentation and analysis of "On Karamlish," an *onītha* written by Gewargis Warda written one year after the November 1237/8 invasion of Northern Mesopotamia. An English translation of the poem is appended to afford scholars access to the primary account. This poem also, in turn, elucidates an understanding that the East Syrian Christians from this region were not, contrary to certain suggestions, spared by the Mongol incursions. The poem presents a view of the activity of the Mongols in Erbil, Karamlish, Bet Qoqa, and Tesqopa. Gewargis Warda's *onītha* provides the most details on the narrative of events in the Nineveh Plains and Erbil during the Mongol incursions and constitutes the principal focus of this article.

Moreover, Bar Hebraeus (d. 1286), the Maphrien of the Syriac Orthodox Church, also furnishes a pivotal account of the invasions in his *Secular History*. He affirms the validity of Warda's narrative, in stating as following:

> In the year 633 of the Arab calendar, Malik Nasir Dawoud, the Lord of Karak and descendant of Mu'tam and Adil, travelled to Baghdad. He went to lodge a complaint with the Caliph against his uncles Kamil and Ashraf, who had seized Damascus from him. The same year, Rukan al-Din Malik Salih Isma'el, the Lord of Mosul and son of Badr-al-Din, also went to Baghdad to serve the Caliph. During this time, Tartar forces reached Erbil and then proceeded to Nineveh. They set up camp near the canal of the village of Karamlish. The residents fled to the church for refuge. Tartar troops captured the church and positioned two nobles at its two doors. One noble spared and released those who exited through his door, while the other slaughtered the men, women, and chil-

dren who left through his door.[22] [my translation]

ܘܒܫܢܬ ܫܬܡܐܐ ܘܬܠܬܝܢ ܘܬܠܬ
ܕܛܝ̈ܝܐ ܐܬܐ ܡܠܟܐ ܢܟܝܪ ܕܐܘܪ̇ܕ ܒܪ
ܡܘܟܠܐ ܒܪ ܟܐܪܠ ܡܪܐ ܕܒܪܟ
ܠܟܢܕܐ ܠܗܬ ܟܠܝܬܗ: ܠܡܣܒܠ ܟܠ
ܕܕ̈ܘܗܝ، ܟܐܡܠ ܘܐܫܪܦ ܕܣܠܩܘ ܡܢܗ
ܕܪܘܡܝܘ. ܘܒܗ ܒܥ̈ܪܬܐ ܬܘܒ ܐܦ
ܪܘܡ ܐܠܝܡ ܡܠܟܐ ܕܐܠܗ
ܐܣܛܡܟܠ ܒܪ ܒܕܪ ܐܠܝܡ ܡܪܐ
ܕܡܢ ܠ ܐܬܐ ܠܟܢܕܐ ܒܬܫܥܝܬܐ
ܕܟܠܝܬܗ. ܘܒܗ ܒܥܒܪܐ ܡܟܠܗ ܬܬ̈ܪܝܐ
ܠܐܪܒܠ: ܘܡܢ ܬܘܡܢ ܐܬܦܐ ܠܫܘܢܐ:
ܘܫܪܐ ܟܠ ܪ̈ܓܠܬܐ ܕܡܪܢܐ ܕܒܪܥܠܫ
ܦܪܬܐ. ܘܟܪܘܘ ܒܗ ܘܟܠܗ ܠܟܢܕܐ
ܕܟܗ̇. ܘܟܟܫܘܗ̇ ܬܬ̈ܪܝܐ ܠܟܢܕܐ:
ܘܬܪܡ ܘܦܪܘܟܐ ܟܠ ܬ̈ܪܡܘܗܝ ܬ̈ܪܥܗ̇
ܡܬܟܘ. ܘܚܕ ܡܢܗܘܢ ܐܚܝܕ ܘܫܪܪ
ܠܗܘܢ ܕܟܬܪܗ ܢܦܩܘ: ܘܗܘ ܐܣ̄ܪܢܐ
ܒܩܘܡܐ ܦܫܩܐ ܚܙܒ ܠܟܢܕܐ ܘܢܘ̈ܢܐ
ܘܛ̈ܠܝܐ ܕܟܬܪܗ ܢܦܩܘ.

This narrative illustrates a consensus between Bar Hebraeus and Warda regarding the timeframe of the Mongols' incursion in Erbil and the Nineveh Plains. Bar Hebraeus uses the Hijri calendar, 633 AH; Warda uses the Seleucid calendar 1547 GE, both in regards to Erbil and the Nineveh Plains.

However, Bar Hebreaus also adds that the Mongols set up a camp in Karamlish and disrupted the village's water supply.

This article presents and particularly focus on Gewargis Warda's *onītha*, placing it within the broader context of the Mongol invasions, to illuminate the narratives of the period. Beyond Warda, poets such as Khamis bar Qardagh and Gabriel Qamsa, among others, warrant further exploration and attention, having thus far received only minimal scholarly focus. The year 1236/7 witnessed the first Mongol invasion, and one year after, Warda wrote his poem. In autumn of 1236/7, Erbil, Bet Qoqa, and Karamlish were invaded, and, thereafter, the Mongols turned to Tesqopa.

Karamlish became a patriarchal centre, where Patriarch Denḥa II (1336-1381) of the Church of the East transferred the See to this town. It became home for a number of Christian princes, working for the Mongols, including ʻAlā'-al-mulk, the son of Sulṭān-Shāh the deacon, as well as Naṣir-al-dīn and Matta. Perhaps this fame attracted the Mongols to Karamlish, where they perpetrated atrocities to the local population and to ecclesiastical buildings, including the tomb of the martyr Barbara.

Another Poem of Gewargis Warda, On Karamlish: Hail your bosom, come and hear.[23]

ܐܚܪܢܝܬܐ ܕܟܪܡܠܝܫ ܕܥܠܘܗ̇ ܕ ܓܝܘܪܓܝܣ ܘܪܕܐ
ܟܪܡܘ ܠܟܝ ܥܘܒܐ ܘܬܘ ܫܡܥܘ❖

1. In the year one thousand five hundred and forty-seven of the Greek king [= AD 1236/7], there was commotion in all regions, nations and all countries when that evil people came, whose tenacious evilness was more significant than all evils. There was commotion and troubles in seas and dry lands. He came like lightning from that distant land, and every person was harassed.

ܐ. ܫܢܬ ܐܠܦ ܘܚܡܫ ܡܐܐ̈
ܘܐܪܒܥܝܢ ܘܫܒܥ ܠܡܠܟܐ ܕܝܘܢ
ܗܘܐ ܫܓܘܫܝܐ ܒܟܠ ܐܬܪ̈ܘܬ
ܘܒܟܠ ܥܡ̈ܡܝܢ ܘܒܟܠ ܐܘܡ̈ܘܬ ܟܕ ܗܘ
ܐܬܐ ܥܡܐ ܒܝܫܐ ܕܒܝܫܘܬܗ ܒܝܫܐ
ܡܢ ܟܠ ܒܝܫܐ ܗܘܝܐ ܕܗܘܐ ܫܓܘܫܝܐ
ܐܦ ܕܠܘܚܨܐ ܠܝܡܐ ܘܝܒܫܐ ܐܬܐ
ܘܒܪܩܐ ܐܝܟ ܒܪܩܐ ܡܢ ܗ̇ܝ ܐܪܥܐ
ܕܪܚܝܩܐ ܘܟܠ ܒܪ ܢܫܐ ܗܘܐ
ܕܚܘܒܐ ܘܠܒܝܫ ܗܘܐ ܚܒܘܫܝܐ ❖

2. In the year before this one, all the fruits had perished, the trees were as firebrands, and plants were like the dead.

ܒ. ܒܫܢܬܐ ܗ̇ܝ ܕܩܕܡ ܗܕܐ
ܟܠ ܦܐܪ̈ܐ ܗܘܘ ܐܒܝ̈ܕܐ
ܘܐܝܠܢ̈ܐ ܗܘܘ ܐܝܟ ܐܘܕ̈ܐ
ܘܙܪ̈ܥܐ ܗܘܘ ܐܝܟ ܡܝ̈ܬܐ❖

3. At the beginning of the latter *Tišrī* (i.e., November), the first indignation began, and on the fourth day, a rough commotion arose in Erbil.

ܓ. ܒܫܘܪܝܗ ܕܬܫܪܝ، ܐܚܪܝܐ
ܫܪܝ، ܪܘܓܙܐ ܩܕܡܝܐ
ܘܒܝܘܡܐ ܕܒܗ ܐܪܒܥܐ
ܒܐܪܒܝܠ ܗܘܐ ܙܘܥܐ ܩܫܝܐ❖

4. On the New Sunday, all of the churches worshipped, and in which
an *Onītha* proclaims on the onset: *Let us enter in praise*.

ܕ. ܒܚܕ ܒܫܒܐ ܕܒܗ ܚܘܕܬܐ
ܚܕ̈ܝܢ ܟܠܗܝܢ ܥܕ̈ܬܐ
ܘܒܗ ܡܬܐܡܪܐ ܒܪܝܫܝܬܐ
ܕܪܫܗ̇ ܢܥܘܠ ܒܬܘܕܝܬܐ❖

5. On the [same] day, during mass,
they surrounded the graves as mighty angels, but they were angry and irritated demons.

ܗ. ܒܗ ܒܝܘܡܐ ܒܥܕܢ ܐܙ̈ܠܐ
ܚܕܪܘܗ̇ ܠܩܒܘܪܬ ܒܘܪ̈ܐ
ܐܝܟ ܡܠܐܟ̈ܐ ܓܢܒ̈ܪܐ
ܫܐ̈ܕܐ ܪܓܝܙܐ ܘܪܓܝܙܐ❖

6. There, they killed princes—princes, sons of princes. The nobles fell outside, and horsemen (fell) inside the pits.

ܘ. ܬܡܢ ܩܛܠܘ ܠܐܡܝܪ̈ܐ
ܐܡܝܪ̈ܐ ܒܢܝ̈ ܐܡܝܪ̈ܐ
ܦܪ̈ܫܐ ܢܦܠܘ ܒܓܘ ܒܪ̈ܐ
ܐܦ ܪ̈ܟܠܐ ܒܓܘ ܚܦܝ̈ܪܐ❖

7. Bitter cries grew powerful in all the markets of the city, but (the invaders) settled in fields like tigers and lionesses.

ܙ. ܥܫܢܬ ܒܟܝܬܐ ܡܪܝܪܬܐ
ܒܟܠܗܘܢ ܫܘܩ̈ܐ ܕܡܕܝܢ̄ܬܐ
ܘܗܢܘܢ ܫܪܝܢ ܗܘܘ ܒܚܩܠܬܐ
ܐܝܟ ܢܡܪ̈ܐ ܘܐܪ̈ܝܘܬܐ❖

8. On the morning of the second day,
they surrounded Beth-Qoqa as clouds full of gloomy darkness and fire-damaging hail.

ܚ. ܒܨܦܪܗ ܕܝܘܡܐ ܬܪܝܢܐ
ܚܕܪܘ ܠܒܝܬ ܩܘܩܐ ܐܝܟ ܥܢܢܐ
ܕܡܠܝܐ ܚܫܘܟܐ ܘܥܪܦܠܐ
ܘܒܪܕܐ ܘܢܘܪܐ ܡܚܒܠܢܐ ❖

9. There, they killed monks,
and obliterated hermits;
they stripped the ascetics,
as naked babies.

ܛ. ܬܡܢ ܩܛܠܘ ܕܝܪ̈ܝܐ
ܘܐܘܒܕܘ ܗܘܘ ܠܝܚܝ̈ܕܝܐ
ܘܫܠܚܘ ܗܘܘ ܠܢܟܝ̈ܦܐ[24]
ܐܝܟ ܥܘ̈ܠܐ ܥܪ̈ܛܠܝܐ ❖

10. They stripped naked men,
men, along with their colleagues,
colleagues, along with their slacks,
and their trousers and their sandals.

ܝ. ܐܫܠܚܘ ܐܢܘܢ ܠܓܒܪ̈ܝܗܘܢ
ܓܒܪ̈ܝܗܘܢ [221v] ܥܡ ܠܚܒܪ̈ܝܗܘܢ
ܚܒܪ̈ܝܗܘܢ ܘܡܫܪ̈ܟܠܝܗܘܢ
ܡܩ̈ܢܣܝܗܘܢ ܘܡܩ̈ܢܣܝܗܘܢ ❖

11. They already stripped their bodies, which covered their bodies.
They turned the day of their birth into the day of their slaughter.

ܝܐ. ܕܠܐ ܫܠܚܘ ܡܢ ܡܛܘܠ ܦܓܪ̈ܝܗܘܢ
ܕܠܐ ܐܬܪܛܠܘ ܠܡܫܟ̈ܢܝܗܘܢ
ܐܝܟ ܝܘܡܐ ܕܡܘܠܕܗܘܢ
ܥܒܕܘ ܐܢܘܢ ܝܘܡ ܕܢܟܣܬܗܘܢ ❖

12. They broke off the holy sanctuary, turning it into a filthy foot stepping. They did not always strip [them] from their flesh. Instead of sounds of the Holy Spirit, sounds of suffering thundered.

ܝܒ. ܬܒܪܘܗܝ ܠܗܝܟܠܐ ܩܕܝܫܐ
ܘܥܒܕܘܗܝ ܕܘܫܐ ܘܡܛܠܫܐ
ܘܚܠܦ ܩ̈ܠܐ ܕܪܘܚܐ ܩܕܝܫܐ.
ܪܥܡ ܗܘܐ ܒܩ̈ܠܐ ܕܚܫܐ ❖

13. They stripped the glorious and holy reliquaries. They cast the corpses of the deceased; the land fills with holiness.

ܝܓ. ܫܠܚܘ ܗܘܘ ܠܥܒ̈ܝܬܐ
ܡܫܒ̈ܚܬܐ ܘܩܕ̈ܝܫܬܐ
ܘܐܪܡܝܘ ܫ̈ܠܕܐ ܕܡܝ̈ܬܬܐ
ܟܕ ܐܪܥܐ ܡܠܝܐ ܩܕܝܫܘܬܐ ❖

14. They dared to enter the holy of holiness, wherein Sanctus thundered. They took away holy vessels, holy cups and patens.

ܝܕ. ܐܡܪܚܘ ܥܠ ܒܝܬ ܩܘܕܫ ܩܘܕ̈ܫܐ
ܕܒܗ ܪܥܡ ܗܘܐ ܩܕ̈ܝܫܐ
ܘܫܩܠܘ ܡܐܢ̈ܐ ܩܕ̈ܝܫܐ
ܟܣ̈ܐ ܘܦܝܢ̈ܟܐ ܡܩܕ̈ܫܐ ❖

15. In the evening of Tuesday, they passed through the Great Zab, and in Karamlish, filled with love, they caused a great terror.

ܝܗ. ܒܪܡܫܐ ܕܬܠܬܐ ܒܫܒܐ
ܥܒܪܘ ܠܗܘܢ ܙܒܐ ܪܒܐ
ܘܒܟܪܡܠܝܫ ܡܠܝܬ ܚܘܒܐ
ܥܒܕܘ ܗܘܘ ܒܗ̇ ܠܚܘܫܐ ܪܒܐ ❖

16. In the evening, there was weeping, and the night did not know sleeping. In the morning, the lamentations thundered, along with cries and screaming.

ܝܘ. ܒܪܡܫܐ ܒܟܬ ܒܒܟܬܐ
ܒܠܠܝܐ ܠܐ ܝܕܥܬ ܫܢܬܐ
ܒܨܦܪܐ ܪܥܡ ܒܗ ܐܘܠܝܬܐ
ܘܩܒܬܐ ܘܙܥܩܬܐ ܀

17. In the evening, daughters dwelled with their mothers in their houses, and so too fathers with their sons and brothers and with them the sisters.

ܝܙ. ܒܪܡܫܐ ܥܡܪܝܢ ܗܘܘ ܒܒܬܝܗܘܢ
ܒܢܬܐ ܠܘܬ ܡܠܕ̈ܬܗܘܢ
ܘܐܒܗ̈ܐ ܥܡ ܝܠܕ̈ܝܗܘܢ
ܘܐܚ̈ܐ ܘܥܡܗܘܢ ܐܚܘ̈ܬܗܘܢ ܀

18. Before morning, they came against them, and killing began suddenly against them; no fathers with their sons nor brothers with their brothers.

ܝܚ. ܩܕܡ ܕܢ ܨܦܪܐ ܡܛܐ ܥܠܝܗܘܢ
ܡܢ ܡܠܟܐ ܟܠܗ ܗܘܐ ܥܠܝܗܘܢ
ܠܐ ܐܒܗ̈ܐ ܠܘܬ ܒܢܝ̈ܗܘܢ
ܘܠܐ ܐܚ̈ܐ ܠܘܬ ܐܚܝ̈ܗܘܢ ܀

19. In the evening, there were grooms and brides, along with chaste men and virgin women. In the morning, there was mourning and sorrow over the departed and the tainted.

ܝܛ. ܒܪܡܫܐ ܚ̈ܬܢܐ ܘܟܠ̈ܠܬܐ
ܘܒ̈ܬܘܠܐ ܘܒ̈ܬܘܠܬܐ
ܒܨܦܪܐ ܐܒ̈ܠܐ ܘܡܪ̈ܝܪܬܐ
ܥܠ ܩ̈ܛܝܠܐ ܘܥܠ ܡܣ̈ܬܠܬܐ ܀

20. In the evening, it [i.e., Karamlish] was teeming with crowds, and, like a sea, it had become troubled. But in the morning, it was filled with the departed, and the groaning did not cease.

ܟ. ܒܪܡܫܐ ܒܟܢܫܐ ܡܠܝܐ ܗܘܬ
ܘܐܝܟ ܝܡܐ ܡܫܓܫܬ ܥܟܝܪܐ ܗܘܬ
ܒܨܦܪܐ ܩ̈ܛܝܠܐ ܡܠܝܐ ܗܘܬ
ܘܝܒܒܐ ܗܘܬ ܘܠܐ ܫܠܝܐ ܗܘܬ ܀

21. In the evening, they [i.e., Karamlishites] wore fine apparel of purple and scarlets, but in the morning, they resembled beasts: naked and dishevelled.

ܟܐ. ܒܪܡܫܐ ܠܒܝܫܝܢ ܬܟܫܝܛܬܐ
ܕܐܪܓܘܢܐ ܘܙܚܘܪ̈ܝܬܐ
ܒܨܦܪܐ ܕܡܝܢ ܠܚܝ̈ܘܬܐ
ܥܪ̈ܛܠܝܬܐ ܘܦܪ̈ܝܥܬܐ ܀

22 In the evening, there were resources in their houses and wine in their cellars. But in the morning, their dwellings were destroyed, and their bedrooms were uprooted.

ܟܒ. ܒܪܡܫܐ ܦܘܪ̈ܢܣܐ ܒܒ̈ܬܝܗܘܢ
ܘܚܡܪܐ ܒܝܬ ܡܕ̈ܢܝܗܘܢ [25]
ܒܨܦܪܐ ܚܪܝܒܝܢ ܡܥܡܪ̈ܝܗܘܢ
ܘܥܩܝܪܝܢ ܡܫܟܘ̈ܢܝܗܘܢ ܀

23. There was not a house where [at least] one did not perish, not one, nor two, nor three. And for those whose lives were spared, their story passes to the word.

ܟܓ. ܠܝܬ ܒܝܬܐ ܕܠܝܬ ܒܗ ܡܝܬܐ
ܠܐ ܚܕ ܘܬܪܝܢ ܘܬܠܬܐ
ܘܐܝܠܝܢ ܕܫܒܩܘ ܒܚܝܘܬܐ
ܒܒܪܐ ܬܫܥܝܬܗܘܢ ܠܡܠܬܐ ܀
[R222]

24. There, honourable men perished, and the fairest of the fair were defiled. And they threw the bodies of heroes, resembling straw beneath threshing sleds.

ܟܕ. ܬܡܢ ܐܒܕܘ ܡܝܩܪܐ
ܘܣܚܠܘ ܫܘܦܪܐ ܕܫܦܝܪܐ
ܘܪܡܘ ܦܓܪܐ ܕܓܢܒܪܐ
ܕܕܡܘܬ ܬܒܢܐ ܬܚܝܬ ܓܪ ܓܪܐ܀

25. Every house was in mourning, others in lamentation. All cried out and raised their voices, but there was no one to hear and none to respond.

ܟܗ. ܟܠ ܒܝܬܐ ܒܟܒܘܗ ܐܒܠܬܗ
ܘܐܚܪܢܐ ܒܟܒܘܗ ܡܐܠܬܗ
ܟܠܗ ܒܟܘ ܘܪܡ ܩܠܗ
ܘܠܝܬ ܕܫܡܥ ܘܠܐ ܕܥܢܐ ܠܗ܀

26. Even loving parents with great love, when they saw the indignation consuming them, left their children and fled from their homes.

ܟܘ. ܐܦ ܐܒܗܐ ܪܒ ܚܘܒܗܘܢ
ܟܕ ܚܙܘ ܪܘܓܙܐ ܕܐܟܠ ܒܗܘܢ
ܐܪܦܝܘ ܘܫܒܩܘ ܠܒܢܝܗܘܢ
ܘܥܪܩܘ ܗܘܘ ܡܢ ܒܬܝܗܘܢ܀

27. The brother abandoned his brother and, out of fear, ran away. The husband left his wife, proceeding straightway ahead.

ܟܙ. ܐܚܐ ܠܐܚܘܗܝ ܫܒܩ ܗܘܐ
ܘܡܢ ܕܚܠܬܗ ܥܪܩ ܗܘܐ
ܘܓܒܪܐ ܠܐܢܬܬܗ ܡܪܦܐ ܗܘܐ
ܘܠܩܘܒܠ ܐܦܘܗܝ ܢܦܩ ܗܘܐ܀

28. With lanterns, they would approach them. Taking the youth captive, they would kill the elders and violate the women.

ܟܚ. ܒܫܪܓܐ ܩܪܝܒ ܗܘܘ ܠܗܘܢ
ܕܠܒܘܪ ܫܒܝܢ ܗܘܘ ܠܗܘܢ
ܘܕܣܒܝܢ ܡܩܛܠܝܢ ܗܘܘ ܠܗܘܢ
ܘܢܫܐ ܬܘܒ ܡܛܢܦܝܢ ܗܘܘ ܒܗܘܢ܀

29. Oh, Karamlishites, they were aloft. They were leaders and wealthy; they were proud and haughty, and they were beautiful and elegant.

ܟܛ. ܘܝ ܟܪܡܠܫܝܐ ܕܪܡܝܢ ܗܘܘ
ܘܪܫܝܢ ܘܥܬܝܪܝܢ ܗܘܘ
ܘܫܒܝܚܝܢ ܘܡܫܬܒܗܪܝܢ ܗܘܘ
ܘܫܦܝܪܝܢ ܘܡܨܒܬܝܢ ܗܘܘ܀

30. The wealthy were made poor, the haughty were humbled, and when the leaders were summoned, they were scorned and insulted!

ܠ. ܥܬܝܪܐ ܗܘܘ ܡܣܟܢܐ
ܘܡܫܬܒܗܪܢܐ ܡܬܡܟܟܢܐ
ܘܡܬܩܪܝܢ ܗܘܘ ܪܝܫܢܐ
ܗܘܘ ܫܝܛܐ ܘܡܚܝ ܠܓܕܦܐ܀

31. Their houses were ample, and their rooms filled. But in a single night, they became impoverished, and not a single survivor was cast out.

ܠܐ. ܕܪܘܝܚܝܢ ܗܘܘ ܒܬܝܗܘܢ
ܘܡܠܝܢ ܗܘܘ ܬܘܢܝܗܘܢ
ܒܚܕ ܠܠܝܐ ܡܣܟܢܘ ܐܟܘ
ܘܦܠܝܛܐ ܠܐ ܐܦܩܘ ܠܗܘܢ܀

32. First, they seized their belongings, their vessels, and their clothing; then, their children, and again their wives, making a mockery of them before them.

ܠܒ. ܫܩܠܘ ܠܘܩܕܡ ܩܢܝܢܗܘܢ
ܘܡܐܢܝܗܘܢ ܘܠܒܘܫܝܗܘܢ
ܘܡܢ ܒܢܝܗܘܢ ܘܬܘܒ ܢܫܝ̈ܗܘܢ
ܘܒܙܚܘ ܠܘܩܒܠ ܥܝܢܝܗܘܢ❖

33. There are those who, driven by fear, fled, while others surrendered themselves. When the killers saw the beautiful ones, they were mocked.

ܠܓ. ܐܝܬ ܕܡܢ ܕܚܠܬܐ ܥܪܩܝܢ ܗ̄ܘܘ
ܘܐܝܬ ܕܢܦܫ̈ܗܘܢ ܡܫܠܡܝܢ ܗ̄ܘܘ
ܠܩܛܘܠܐ ܟܕ ܚܙܝܢ ܗ̄ܘܘ
ܫܦܝ̈ܪܐ ܕܡܬܒܙܚܝܢ ܗ̄ܘܘ❖

34. Oh! Oh! How terrifying the evening was! Ah! Ah! How confusing the night was! Woah! Woah! How tumultuous the morning was! How rough and chaotic it became!

ܠܕ. ܐܘܗ̇ ܐܘܗ̇ ܪܡܫܐ ܟܡܐ ܕܚܝܠ ܗ̄ܘܐ
ܐܘܝ, ܐܘܝ, ܠܠܝܐ ܟܡܐ ܒܠܒܠ ܗ̄ܘܐ
ܘ̈ܝ, ܘ̈ܝ ܨܦܪܐ ܟܡܐ ܒܥܫ ܗ̄ܘܐ
ܟܡܐ ܩܫܐ ܗ̄ܘܐ ܘܟܡܐ ܫܓܝܫ ܗ̄ܘܐ❖

35. In the evening, evil entered it; by night, evil over evil. Its splendour was trampled, and its tranquillity became disrupted.

ܠܗ. ܒܪܡܫܐ ܥܠܬ ܠܗ̇ ܒܝܫܬܐ
ܒܠܠܝܐ ܒܝܫܬܐ ܥܠ ܒܝܫܬܐ
ܪܘܪܒܘܬܐ ܗܘܬ ܠܗ̇ ܕܫܝܫܬܐ
ܘܫܝܢܘܬܐ ܗܘܬ ܫܓܝܫܬܐ❖

36. When they ravaged the village, they left it entirely as ruins. In the morning, a great crowd arrived, obliterating [both] the young and the old.

ܠܘ. ܟܕ ܒܙܘ ܒܩܪܝܬܐ ܚܪܒܐ
ܘܫܒܩܘܗ̇ ܟܠܗ̇ ܐܝܟ ܚܪܒܐ
ܡܛܐ ܒܨܦܪܐ ܟܢܫܐ ܪܒܐ
ܘܐܘܒܕܘ ܠܙܥܘܪܐ ܥܡ ܪܒܐ❖

37. They forced their way into the sacred Church, turning it into a tavern to be trampled upon. What was once glorious became a dreadful mockery.

ܠܙ. ܬܪܨܘܗ̇ ܠܒܝܬܐ [222r] ܩܕܝܫܬܐ
ܘܥܒܕܘܗ̇ ܐܝܟ ܦܘܬܩܐ ܕܫܝܫܬܐ
ܘܚܠܦ ܕܐܝܬܝܗ̇ ܗ̄ܘܬ ܫܒܝܚܬܐ
ܗܘܬ ܡܒܙܚܬܐ ܘ ܚܒܝܫܬܐ❖

38. They spilled blood like a flood, and tears flowed like waves. Cries resounded, rising because of the killers and the slain.

ܠܚ. ܒܒܕܘ ܒܗ̇ ܕܡܐ ܐܝܟ ܡܛܘ̈ܠܐ
ܘܕܡ̈ܥܐ ܒܕܡܘܬ ܡܫܘ̈ܠܐ
ܕ̈ܒܟܝܢ ܗ̄ܘܘ ܘܣܠܩܝܢ ܩ̈ܠܐ
ܕܩܛܘ̈ܠܐ ܐܦ ܕܩܛܝ̈ܠܐ❖

39. The Tartars roared as tigers against the poor Karamlishites. They bellowed and fell like frightened children before their captors.

ܠܛ. ܐܝܟ ܢܡܪ̈ܐ ܢܗܡܘ ܛܛܪ̈ܝܐ
ܥܠ ܡܣܟ̈ܢܐ ܟܪ̈ܡܫܝܐ
ܘܢܗܡܘ ܘܢܦܠܘ ܐܝܟ ܛܠ̈ܝܐ
ܡܢ ܕܚܠܬܐ ܕܫܒ̈ܝܐ❖

40. No man saved his wife, nor did the father save his daughter. No brother rescued his sister, for everyone was overcome by fear.

ܡ. ܠܐ ܓܒܪܐ ܦܪܩܗ̇ ܠܐܢܬܬܗ
ܘܠܐ ܐܒܐ ܫܘܙܒ ܒܪܬܗ
ܘܠܐ ܐܚܐ ܦܨܝ, ܚܬܗ
ܕܟܠܢܫ ܚܕ ܡܢ ܕܚܠܬܗ❖

41. They entered into the house of worship, splendid and glorious, and turned it into [a place] to be trampled upon, like adulterous beasts.	ܡܐ. ܥܠܘ ܗܘܘ ܠܓܘ ܒܝܬ ܨܠܘ̈ܬܐ ܬܡܝܗܬܐ ܘܡܫܒܚܬܐ ܘܥܒܕܘ ܐܢܝ ܡܬܠܓܫܬܐ ܐܝܟ ܚܝܘ̈ܬܐ ܕܙܢܝܘܬܐ ❖
42. They did not have mercy on the virgins, nor did they spare young girls. They disrobed them and treated them disgracefully, like cornered prostitutes.	ܡܒ. ܠܐ ܪܚܡܘ ܥܠ ܒܬܘ̈ܠܬܐ ܘܠܐ ܚܣܘ ܗܘܘ̈ ܥܠ ܥܠܝ̈ܡܬܐ ܐܫܠܚܘ ܘܐܦܩܘ ܠܒܗܬܬܐ ܐܝܟ ܙܢܝ̈ܬܐ ܒܙܘ̈ܝܬܐ ❖
43. Mockery and captivity prevailed, and exposing shame. Cries and lamentation resounded, with tears flowing like water.	ܡܓ. ܥܫܢܘ ܒܓܘܗ̇ ܒܘܙܚܐ ܘܫܒܝܐ ܘܦܪܣܝܐ ܕܠܐ ܒܗܬܬܐ ܘܪܓܫ ܗܘܐ ܒܟܝܐ ܘܐܠܝܐ ܘܢܬܪܝ ܕܡ̈ܥܐ ܐܝܟ ܡ̈ܝܐ ❖
44. They took captive their handsome men and seized the young. Their format resembled lambs before their slaughters.	ܡܕ. ܫܒܘ ܐܢܘܢ ܠܫܦܝܪ̈ܝܗܘܢ ܘܐܚܕܘ ܗܘܘ̈ ܠܥܠܝ̈ܡܝܗܘܢ ܟܕ ܕܡܝܢ ܗܘܘ̈ ܐܣܟܡ̈ܝܗܘܢ ܠܐܡܪ̈ܐ ܩܕܡ ܠܢܟܣ̈ܝܗܘܢ ❖
45. They divided them into two divisions, separating them into two parts: One part was killed, while the other was left to live.	ܡܗ. ܦܠܓܘܗ̇ ܠܬܪ̈ܬܝܢ ܦܠܓܘ̈ܬܐ ܘܥܒܕܘܗ̇ ܬܪ̈ܬܝܢ ܡܢܘ̈ܬܐ ܘܠܩܛܠܐ ܚܕܐ ܦܠܓܘܬܐ ܗܘܬ ܘܐܚܪܬܐ ܠܫܒܩܬܐ ❖
46. One Tartar prince, standing at the eastern gate, had little fear of the Lord; to his group, he granted deliverance.	ܡܘ. ܚܕ ܐܡܝܪܐ ܛܛܪܝܐ ܩܡ ܒܬܪܥܐ ܡܕܢܚܝܐ ܕܚܠ ܗܘܐ ܩܠܝܠ ܡܢ ܡܪܝܐ ܠܓܒܬܗ ܝܗܒ ܦܘܨܝܐ ❖
47. The one at the southern gate rendered killing over captivity, and he had no mercy on the child nor on the becoming parent.	ܡܙ. ܗܘ̇ ܕܒܬܪܥܐ ܬܝܡܢܝܐ ܐܘܣܦ ܩܛܠܐ ܥܠ ܫܒܝܐ ܘܠܐ ܪܚܡ ܠܐ ܥܠ ܛܠܝܐ ܘܠܐ ܥܠ ܝܠܘܕܐ ܦܐܝܐ ❖
48. There, they killed priests and the esteemed ranks of deacons. Honourable bodies were trampled, resembling dry leaves.	ܡܚ. ܬܡܢ ܩܛܠܘ ܩܫܝ̈ܫܐ ܘܣܕ̈ܪܐ ܪ̈ܫܝܐ ܕܫܡ̈ܫܐ ܘܦܓܪ̈ܐ ܡܝܩܪ̈ܐ ܗܘܘ ܕܝܫ̈ܐ ܒܕܡܘܬ ܛܪ̈ܦܐ ܝܒܝ̈ܫܐ ❖
49. "O Church, remain in peace," was not chanted on that day. They did not start with "remain in peace," nor could they respond with "go in peace."	ܡܛ. ܥܕܬܐ ܦܘܫ ܠܟܝ ܒܫܠܡܐ ܠܐ ܐܬܐܡܪܬ ܒܗ̇ܘ ܝܘܡܐ ܠܐ ܫܪܝܘ ܦܘܫ ܒܫܠܡܐ ܘܠܐ ܥܢܘ ܙܠܘ ܒܫܠܡܐ ❖

50. “Woe! Woe! Oh! Oh! Oh!,” the mothers cried out over their daughters who had been violated and for themselves who were mocked.

ܢ. ܘܝ̈، ܘܝ̈، ܐܘ̈، ܐܘ̈، ܐܘ̈،
ܐܡ̈ܗܬܐ ܩܥ̈ܝܢ ܗ̄ܘ̈ܝ،
ܘܥܠ ܒܢ̈ܬܐ ܕܡܛܢ̈ܦܢ ܗ̄ܘ̈ܝ،
ܘܥܠ ܢܦܫ̈ܬܗܝܢ ܕܒܙܚܐ ܗܘ̈ܝ، ❖ [223r]

51. They slaughtered their sons upon their chests and their husbands before their eyes. Their bodies were dishonoured, and their assailants mocked them.

ܢܐ. ܕܒܚܘ ܒܢ̈ܝܗܝܢ ܒܥܘ̈ܒܝܗܝܢ
ܘܓܒܪ̈ܝܗܝܢ ܩܕܡ ܥܝ̈ܢܝܗܝܢ
ܘܐܬܛܠܫ ܠܦܓ̈ܪܝܗܝܢ
ܘܒܙܚܘ ܒܗܝܢ ܫܒ̈ܒܝܗܝܢ ❖

52. Now, whom do I mourn for? And whom do I not? The wound has befallen the domain of the villagers, who are now without number.

ܢܒ. ܥܠ ܐܝܢܐ ܗܘ ܒܟܐ ܐܢܐ
ܘܥܠ ܐܝܢܐ ܠܐ ܒܟܐ ܐܢܐ
ܕܡܚܘܬܐ ܡܛܬ ܠܐܘܪܢܐ
ܕܩܘܪ̈ܝܐ ܕܠܝܬ ܠܗܘܢ ܡܢܝܢܐ ❖

53. Now, which of them do I lament? And which of them do I not? Over the countless ones slain or the captors who are beyond number?

ܢܓ. ܥܠ ܐܝܠܝܢ ܗܘ ܐܠܐ ܐܢܐ
ܘܥܠ ܐܝܠܝܢ ܠܐ ܐܠܐ ܐܢܐ
ܥܠ ܩ̈ܛܝܠܐ ܕܠܐ ܡܢܝܢܐ
ܐܘ ܫܒܝ̈ܐ ܕܠܐ ܚܘܫܒܢܐ ❖

54. I will mourn over Tesqopa a great and powerful village! Like a bird with a clipped wing, one church was eradicated by the sword.

ܢܕ. ܒܟܐ ܐܢܐ ܠܬܠܐ ܐܣܩܘܦܐ
ܩܪܝܬܐ ܪܒܬܐ ܕܬܘܩܦܐ
ܕܐܝܟ ܦܪܚܐ ܡܦܣ̱ܩܬ ܓܦܐ
ܚܕܐ ܥܕܬܐ ܦܣܩܬ ܒܣܝܦܐ ❖

55. The Church of Mār James the Intercisus: How grievously it suffered! It lamented in agony, and no saviour came to it.

ܢܗ. ܥܕܬܐ ܕܡܪܝ، ܝܥܩܘܒ ܡܦܣܩܐ
ܐܝܟ ܥܠ ܠܗ̇ ܦܣܩܐ
ܘܗܘܬ ܒܟܝܐ ܘܡܬܬܢܚܐ
ܘܠܐ ܐܬܐ ܠܗ̇ ܦܪܘܩܐ ❖

56. Those who were slain and [now] lie in tombs are better off than those taken captive and imprisoned. For they (i.e., former) rest in graveyards, and these [latter ones] live in bitterness.

ܢܘ. ܛܒܝܢ ܗ̄ܘܘ ܩ̈ܛܝܠܐ ܡܩܒܪ̈ܐ
ܡܢ ܫܒܝ̈ܐ ܘܡܢ ܐܣܝܪ̈ܐ
ܕܗ̇ܢܘܢ ܢܝܚܝܢ ܒܒܝܬ ܡܩܒܪ̈ܐ
ܘܗܠܝܢ ܚܝܝܢ ܒܡܪ̈ܝܪܐ ❖

57. If they hunger, there is no one to feed them; if they are thirsty, there is no one to quench their thirst. Due to the intensity of their sufferings, even sleep eludes them.

ܢܙ. ܐܢ ܟܦܢܝܢ ܠܝܬ ܕܡܘܟܠ ܠܗܘܢ
ܘܐܢ ܨܗܝܢ ܠܝܬ ܕܡܫܩܐ ܠܗܘܢ
ܘܡܢ ܥܫܝܢܘܬ ܛܘܪ̈ܦܝܗܘܢ
ܐܦܠܐ ܫܢܬܐ ܐܬܝܐ ܠܗܘܢ ❖

58. They were naked with no one to clothe them. They yearned for mere crumbs of bread; these were roughly given. And if they should stumble and fall, woe to them!	ܢܚ. ܥܪܛܠܝܢ ܘܠܝܬ ܕܡܟܣܐ ܠܗܘܢ ܘܪ̈ܓܬܐ ܕܠܚܡܐ ܪ ܟܐ ܠܗܘܢ ܡܫܬܐܠܬ ܡܪܗ̄ܛܠܝ ܠܗܘܢ ܘܐܢ ܬܬܩܠܝܢ ܘܢܦܠܝܢ ܘܝ ܠܗܘܢ ❖
59. Buyers were unfamiliar to them; they did not have sellers. They moved on and departed their homes, much like the dead in their graves.	ܢܛ. ܙܒܘܢܐ ܠܐ ܝܕܥܝܢ ܠܗܘܢ ܡܙܒܢܢܐ ܠܐ ܗܘܘ ܠܗܘܢ ܢܦܩܘ ܘܐܙܠܘ ܡܢ ܒܬ̈ܝܗܘܢ[26] ܐܝܟ ܡ̈ܝܬܐ ܕܠܩܒܪ̈ܝܗܘܢ ❖
60. Not in the feast of the Nativity did they celebrate, nor in Epiphany were they baptized. Not during the fifty days of fasting did they abstain, nor with the assemblies of the faithful did they mingle.	ܣ. ܠܐ ܒܥܐܕܐ ܕܝܠܕܐ ܪܘܙܘ ܘܠܐ ܒܥܐܕܐ ܕܕܢܚܐ ܐܬܥܡܕܘ ܘܠܐ ܒܨܘܡܐ ܕܚܡܫܝܢ ܨܡܘ ܘܠܐ ܥܡ ܡܗܝܡ̈ܢܐ ܐܬܚܠܛܘ ❖
61. They did not come out to exalt on the day of Hosanna, nor in the thought of the Resurrection Day did their hearts dwell- on this day, none reminded them.	ܣܐ. ܠܐ ܢܦܩܘ ܒܝܘܡ ܐܘܫܥܢܐ ܘܠܐ ܩ̇ܘܡ ܠܗܘܢ ܡܚܫܒܢܐ ܘܒܗ ܡܥܡܪܬܐ ܠܒܗܘܢ ܪܢܐ ܟܠ ܡܥܡܪܬܐ ܕܠܝܬ ܡܥܗܕܢܐ ❖
62. They remained unaware of any feasts and neither any festivals. They did not hear the sounds of Sunday; [instead] they drank their tears, yet found no satisfaction.	ܣܒ. ܐܝܟ ܒܥܐܕܐ ܕܠܐ ܝܕܥܝܢ ܘܒܥܐܕܐ ܕܠܐ ܡܫܬܘܕܥܝܢ ܘܠ ܚܕ ܒܫܒܐ ܠܐ ܫܡܥܝܢ ܘܫܬܝܢ ܕܡ̈ܥܐ ܘܠܐ ܣܒܥܝܢ ❖
63. Oh Lord of lords, where is the parable, which is in your vivifying Gospel, about your chosen wheat?	ܣܓ. ܐܘ ܡܪܐ ܡܪ̈ܘܬܐ ܐܝܟܐ ܗ̄ܝ ܕܒܗ ܦܠܐܬܐ ܕܒܣܒܪܬܟ ܡܚܝܢܝܬܐ[358r[27]] ܡܛܠ ܚܛܬܐ ܓܒܝܬܐ ❖
64. You, O Lord, commanded the winds to spare the wheat—royal offspring— for the sake of the wheat, the children of the faithful.	ܣܕ. ܐܢܬ ܡܪܝ ܦܩܕܬ ܠܪ̈ܘܚܐ ܕܠܐ ܢܗܘܘܢ ܠܗܘܢ ܡܚܒܠܢܐ ܠܚܛܬܐ ܒܢ̈ܝ ܡܠܟܐ ܒܥܠܬ ܚܛܬܐ ܒܢ̈ܝ ܡܗܝܡ̈ܢܐ ❖
65. Behold! The weeds have grown powerful, and the roots of the wheat have been uprooted! O, judge over all judges, from those whom these are judging.	ܣܗ. ܗܐ ܙܝܙܢܐ ܥܫܝܢ ܘܚܛܬܐ ܥܩ̈ܪܝܗ̇ܝ ܥܩܝܪܝܢ ܐܘ ܕܝܢܐ ܥܠ ܕܝܢܝܢ ܡܢ ܐܝܠܝܢ ܗܠܝܢ ܕܕܝܢܝܢ ❖
66. If the churches are uprooted and the monasteries and convents demolished, what then is the edict of this blasphemy, and what is the response of baptism?	ܣܘ. ܐܢ ܡܬܥܩ̈ܪܢ ܥܕ̈ܬܐ ܘܣܚܝܦܝܢ ܥܘܡܪ̈ܐ ܘܕܝܪ̈ܬܐ ܡܢ ܐܡܪܐ ܟܦܘܪܬܐ ܘܡܢ ܥܢܝܐ ܡܥܡܘܕܝܬܐ[28]

67. The hidden mind awoke me and said to me: "Silence, O wretched one! Your question is loathsome, even more so than your hateful person!"

ܣܙ. ܐܬܬܥܝܪ ܥܠܝ ܗܘܢܐ ܟܣܝܐ
ܘܐܡܪ ܠܝ ܫܬܘܩ ܐܘ ܕܘܝܐ
ܫܐܠܬܟ ܐܣܬܘܗܝ ܣܢܝܐ
ܘܣܢܝܐ ܡܢ ܩܢܘܡܟ ܣܢܝܐ ❖

68. "Have you not heard what your Lord said to all the faithful: 'They will hate you and kill you, and offer you as sacrifices.

ܣܚ. ܠܐ ܫܡܥܬ ܡܪܟ ܐܡܪ ܠܗܘܢ
ܡܪܟ ܠܡܗܝܡ̈ܢܐ ܟܠܗܘܢ
ܕܣܢܝܢ ܠܟܘܢ ܘܡܩܛܠܝܢ ܠܟܘܢ
ܘܐܝܟ ܩܘܪ̈ܒܢܐ ܡܩܪܒܝܢ ܠܟܘܢ ❖

69. I shall send you like lambs among the wolves so that they will strangle you! When they kill you in the earth, you will rejoice in my Kingdom with me!

ܣܛ. ܘܐܝܟ ܐܡܪ̈ܐ ܡܫܕܪܢܐ ܠܟܘܢ ܒܝܢ̈ܬ
ܕܐܒ̈ܐ ܕܢܚܢܩܘܢ ܠܟܘܢ
ܘܟܕ ܒܐܪܥܐ ܡܬܩܛܠܝܬܘܢ[29]
ܒܡܠܟܘܬܝ، ܥܡܝ ܡܬܒܣܡܝܬܘܢ[30] ❖

70. The servant is not above his lord, nor is the messenger greater than the one who sent him. Your Lord was killed, and His tomb sealed, yet your mouth persists in its idle chatter!

ܥ. ܘܠܐ ܥܒܕܐ ܠܥܠ ܡܢ ܡܪܗ
ܘܠܐ ܫܠܝܚܐ ܪܒ ܡܢ ܕܫܕܪܗ
ܡܪܟ ܐܬܩܛܠ ܘܚܬܝܡ ܩܒܪܗ
ܘܐܢܬ ܦܘܡܟ ܒܥܝܢ ܗܦܪܗ ❖

71. There are those who are killed for their sins, and I think they are not oppressed. While there are some who do not sin yet have been killed. They shall receive the crown with the martyrs.

ܥܐ. ܐܝܬ ܕܒܚܛܗ̈ܝܗܘܢ ܡܬܩܛܠܝܢ
ܘܣܒܪ ܐܢܐ ܕܠܐ ܡܬܛܠܡܝܢ
ܘܐܝܬ ܕܟܕ ܠܐ ܚܛܘ ܡܬܩܛܠܝܢ
ܥܡ ܣܗ̈ܕܐ ܟܠܝܠܐ ܢܣܒܝܢ ❖

72. Have you not heard that Peter was slain, and among the killed ones perished the head of Paul? Collect your thoughts and restrain yourself! Do not meddle in such matters!

ܥܒ. ܠܐ ܫܡܥܬ ܠܟ ܕܩܛܠܘ ܦܛܪܘܣ
[63v[31]] ܘܒܩܛ̈ܝܠܐ ܐܒܕ ܪܫ ܦܘܠܘܣ
ܐܟܢܫ[32] ܚܘܫܒܝܟ ܘܩܦܘܣ
ܘܒܐܝܟ ܗܠܝܢ ܠܐ ܬܬܗܡܘܣ ❖

73. You have sinned and transgressed as a wrongdoer. As a transgressor, I speak! I speak spiritually! Have mercy on me and the author!

ܥܓ. ܚܛܝܬ ܘܐܣܟܠܬ ܐܝܟ ܡܣܟܠܢܐ
[64r] ܘܐܝܟ ܡܣܟܠܢܐ ܡܡܠܠ ܐܢܐ
ܡܡܠܠ ܐܢܐ ܐܘ ܪܘܚܢܐ
ܪܚܡ ܥܠܝ ܘܥܠ ܡܪܟܒܢܐ ❖

74. Have mercy on the oppressed and those who became diminished in number. Be their guardian and comforter! Praise to you in every tongue, and may Your mercies be upon us at all times.

ܥܕ. ܚܘܣ ܠܛܠܝܡ̈ܐ
ܘܠܒܘܪ̈ܐ ܕܦܫܘ ܒܡܢܝܢܐ
ܡܛܪܢܐ ܘܡܒܝܐܢܐ
ܘܠܟ ܬܫܒܘܚܬܐ ܒܟܠ ܠܫܢܐ
ܘܥܠܝܢ ܪ̈ܚܡܝܟ ܒܟܠ ܙܒܢܐ ❖

Figure 1: Mart Barbara Monastery on Tel Barbara, Karamlish, 2018
(Photo: James Toma)

Figure 2: Bet Qoqa, Church of Mār-Gōrgīs - Upper Section of the Only Gate Leading to the Sanctuary
(Photo: Amir Harrak)

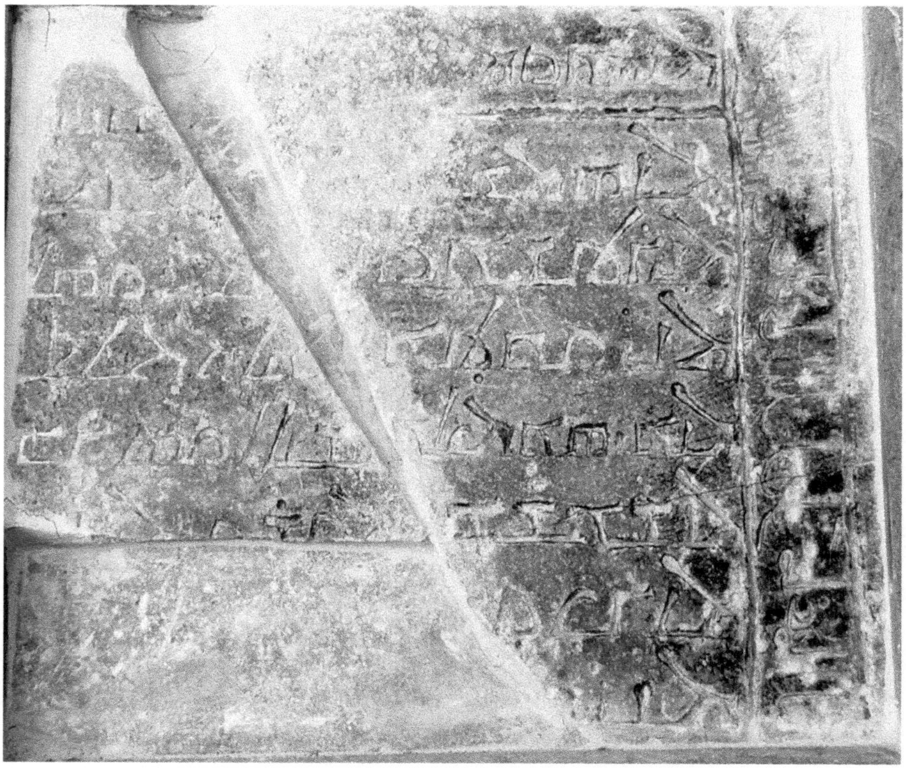

Figure 3: Funerary Inscription of ‘Alā’-al-dīn the deacon (Photo: Amir Harrak)

Figure 4: Baqofa (Bet Qoqa). A Photo Essay of the Homeland
(Photo: Wilson Sarkis). Source: Chaldean News

Figure 5: Mart Barbara Inscription, Karamlish, 2018
(Photo: James Toma)

Figure 6: Mart Barbara Inscription, Karamlish, 2018
(Photo: James Toma)

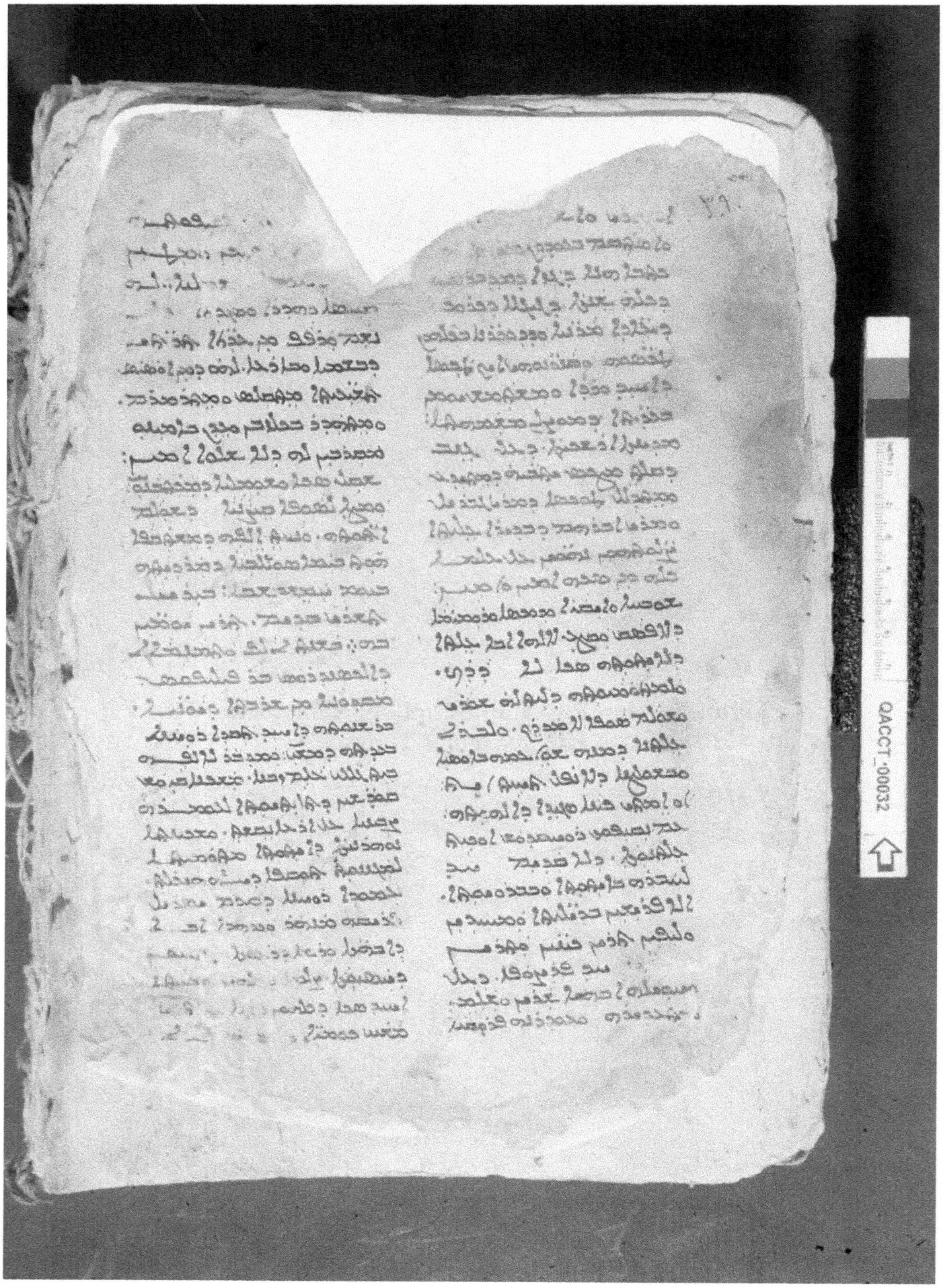

Figure 7: Colophon for Qalb-al-Aqdas Chaldean Church (QACCT) 00032
(By Permission of: Archbishop Najeeb Michaeel al-Sanaty, O. P.)

Figure 8: Inside the Mausoleum of Mart Barbara, Karamlish
(Photo: Amir Harrak)

Figure 9: St. Barbara Well, Karamlish, 2018 (Photo: James Toma)

Figure 10: A View of Tesqopa
(Photo: James Toma)

NOTES

[1]A Mongolian assemblage was held to strategically plan military expeditions. See for more information, David Morgan, *The Mongols,* The Peoples of Europe (Oxford, UK; New York, NY: B. Blackwell, 1986), 61.

[2] Morgan, *The Mongols,* 62-67.

[3] René Grousset, *The Empire of the Steppes; a History of Central Asia,* trans. Naomi Walford (New Brunswick, N.J: Rutgers University Press, 1970), 189.

[4] "In 1218 a caravan of 450 Muslim merchants from Mongol territory arrived at the Khwarazm-shah's frontier city of Utrar. The governor of the city, asserting, no doubt correctly, that these so-called merchants were in fact spies, had them all killed, and their property confiscated. One man is said to have escaped the massacre and to have returned to Chingiz with the tale. Three ambassadors were sent to the Khwarazm-shah to demand reparation and the punishment of the governor of Utrar. The Khwarazm-shah's response was to kill one envoy and – almost as serious an insult – to shave off the beards of the other two [...] in Mongol eyes the person of an ambassador, especially one of their own, was sacrosanct. No reply was possible but war." Morgan, *The Mongols,* 68.

[5] Morris Rossabi, *The Mongols: A Very Short Introduction* (Oxford; New York: Oxford University Press, 2012), 25.

[6] Grousset, 261.

[7] Ibid.

[8] Ibid.

[9] John E. Woods, "A Note on the Mongol Capture of Iṣfahān," *Journal of Near Eastern Studies* 36, no. 1 (Jan. 1977): 49–51

[10] In the Telkeppe collection, three early MSS contain "On Karamlish." These include (1) Qalb al-Aqdas Chaldean Church (QACCT) 00032 (Date: October 2, 1488); (2) QACCT 00035 (Date: August 28, 1686); and (3) QACCT 00036 (Date: March 13, 1689).

For additional details, consult the Telkeppe catalog by Khairy Foumia; see his *Fahras Mukhaṭṭuṭāt Muktabat Kanīsat Tīlkef* (Michigan, 2017), p. 107-119; see also Khairy Foumia, "The Manuscripts of the Church of Telkeppe," *JCSSS* 13 (2013), 66-76. In addition, other manuscripts include Berlin. 65 (Ms. Orient. Fols. 619). Fols. 240r-242v (Date: March 19, 1715). For an important overview of the manuscripts of the Warda's collection more generally, see Anton Pritula, "The Wardā Hymnological Collection," *Patrologia Pacifica Tertia: Selected Papers Presented to the Asia-Pacific Early Christian Studies Society* (Piscataway: Gorgias Press (2013).

[11] Aladár Deutsch, *Edition Dreier Syrischen Lieder nach einer Handschrift der Berliner Königlichen Bibliothek* (Ph.D. diss., University of Bern, 1895; published Berlin: Itzkowski).

[12] Heinrich Hilgenfeld, *Ausgewählte Gesänge Des Giwargis Warda Von Arbel* (Leipzig, 1904).

[13] Pier Giorgio Borbone, "Due episodi delle relazioni tra Mongoli e Siri nel XIII secolo nella storiografia e nella poesia Siriaca," *Egitto e Vicino Oriente* 33 (2010), 205–28.

[14] See Figure 7 for image. The full colophon (39v) reads as follows:

ܫܠܡ ܗܟܐ ܘܫܘܡܠܝܐ ܕܡܟܬܒܢܘܬܗ:
ܘܡܚܝܠܐ ܠܗܘܦܟܐ ܡܢ ܢܝܚܐ ܕܫܘܠܡ
ܐܝܬܘܬܗ. ܘܢܚܬ ܐܠܦܗ ܕܡܬܩܢܘܬܐ
ܗܘܬ ܒܝܘܡ ܚܡܫܒܫܒܐ: ܒܝܪܚ
ܬܫܪܝ ܩܕܝܡ. ܬܪܝܢ ܒܗ ܘܫܢܬ
ܒܗ ❖ ܒܫܢܬ ܐܠܦ ܘܬܡܢܡܐܐ
ܕܐܠܟܣܢܕܪܘܣ ܒܪ ܦܝܠܝܦܘܣ.
ܡܩܕܘܢܝܐ ܡܢ ܫܪܒܬܐ ܕܝܘܢܝܐ.

"The manuscript was bound, completed and arrived at its final edit and shape. For many times over, it went down, had been repaired, and was [complete] on Thursday, in the month of *Tišrī Qdīm* (i.e., October), the second day of it, in the year one thousand and eight hundred of Alexander the son of Philip, the Macedonian from the lineage of the Greeks."

[15] QACCT 00035 and 00036 both contain an addition verse. Whereas, Berlin 65 does not have the additional one.

[16] See for more information Mengozzi, "Gewargis Warda," in *Gewargis Warda*, https://gedsh.bethmardutho.org/Gewargis-Warda. On Warda's work, Rony Beth Yawalaha has catalogued some 177 potential attributions from *The Book of the Rose* in two volumes, see *Kunš mušḥattā d-Gewargis Wardā Arbīlayyā*, 2 vols. (Dohuk, 2014).

[17] See for more information, Mardin, Turkey Chaldean Cathedral (CCM 00396. Folios 208r-210r.

[18] Alessandro Mengozzi, "ʿOnithā," in *ʿOnithā*, edited by Sebastian P. Brock, Aaron M. Butts, George A. Kiraz, and Lucas Van Rompay (Gorgias Press, 2011; online ed. Beth Mardutho, 2018), https://gedsh. beth-mardutho.org/Onitha..

[19] See for more information, Jean Maurice Fiey, *Assyrie Chrétienne* 2 (Beirut: Imprimerie Catholique de Beyrouth, 1975), 379-380.

[20] Amir Harrak, "Karamlish," accessed April 19, 2022: https://gedsh. bethmardutho.org /Karamlish.

[21] John E. Woods, "A Note on the Mongol Capture of Iṣfahān," *Journal of Near Eastern Studies* 36, no. 1 (Jan. 1977): 49–51.

[22] Paul Bedjan, ed., *Gregorii Barhebræi, Chronicon Syriacum e codd. mss. emendatum ac punctis vocalibus adnotationibusque. locupletatum* (Paris: Maisonneuve, 1890), 469.

[23] This prelude is taken from Berlin. 65 Fol. 240r).

[24] Berlin. 65 (Fol. 240v) reads, ܠܡܣܒܪ̈ܢܐ.

[25] Berlin. 65 (Fol. 240v) reads, ܒܝܬ ܩܘ̈ܫܝܗܘܢ.

[26] Berlin. 65 (Fol. 242r) reads, ܕܪ̈ܬܗܘܢ

[27] The second manuscript begins at verse 63 and ends at verse 71. See, QACCT 00035. Fol. 358r.

[28] QACCT 00035 and 00036 both contain this addition verse, which is not available in Berlin 65.

[29] Berlin. 65 (Fol. 240v) reads, ܡܬܩܛܠܝܢ ܐܢܬܘܢ.

[30] Berlin. 65 (Fol. 240v) reads, ܡܬܒܣܡܝܢ ܐܢܬܘܢ.

[31] The final manuscript begins here up to the end, QACCT 00036. Fol. 63v-64r.

[32] Berlin. 65 (Fol. 242v) reads, ܓܒܥ.

Milton Keynes UK
Ingram Content Group UK Ltd.
UKHW051454211024
449815UK00015B/71

9 781463 246198